WARNINGS
AGAINST
MYSELF

DAVID STEVENSON

WARNINGS AGAINST MYSELF

MEDITATIONS ON A LIFE IN CLIMBING

UNIVERSITY OF WASHINGTON PRESS
Seattle and London

Printed and bound in the United States of America
Design by Thomas Eykemans
Composed in Cassia, typeface designed by Dieter Hofrichter
Display type set in Montserrat, designed by Julieta Ulanovsky
20 19 18 17 16   5 4 3 2 1

UNIVERSITY OF WASHINGTON PRESS
www.washington.edu/uwpress

Cataloging information is on file with the Library of Congress
ISBN 978-0-295-99553-3

The paper used in this publication is acid-free and meets the mini-
mum requirements of American National Standard for Information
Sciences—Permanence of Paper for Printed Library Materials,
ANSI Z39.48–1984. ∞

For my sons,

Macklin Stevenson
1993–2015

Slow your roll and hold your own
A million miles, a million roads.
—Macklin Stevenson

and

Dougal Stevenson

Even though we navigate daily through a perceptual world of three spatial dimensions and reason occasionally about higher dimensional arenas with mathematical ease, the world portrayed on our information displays is caught up in the two-dimensionality of the endless flatlands of paper and video screen. All communication between readers of an image and the makers of an image must now take place on a two-dimensional surface. Escaping this flatland is the essential task of envisioning information—for all the interesting worlds (physical, biological, imaginary, human) that we seek to understand are inevitably and happily multivariate in nature. Not flatlands.

—Edward Tufte, *Envisioning Information*

Contents

WARNINGS

AGAINST

MYSELF

INTRODUCTION

Since it is certainly not customary for an author to discuss his own work, perhaps a word of apology, or at least an explanation should occupy first place.
—Thomas Mann, "The Making of
The Magic Mountain," 1953

Warnings against Myself accrued essay by essay over more than twenty-five years, beginning in about 1989. I began climbing in 1971. By 1989, some of the events I was writing about had already been unruly residents in the treasure house of memory for eighteen years.

If taken as a whole, they might be read as a kind of mountaineering memoir. If so, it is one that leaves out enormous amounts of my life, such as my family life and my working life, all of which unfolded in the foreground while my mountaineering life occurred mostly in the margins or waited in the wings.

But I never set out to write a memoir, nor have I done so.

The writing is not chronological, nor necessarily linear. Most of the essays—the ones I like best anyway—might best be described as recursive. I've added as postscripts the year the essays were written and a note from the present reflecting on how they strike me now. The more recent essays require less commentary.

I set out to write literary essays, by which I mean something more sophisticated than a traditional mountaineering trip report. The reports collected in the annual *American Alpine Journal* are models of this traditionally minimalistic and journalistic style. Those reports are usually limited to a single paragraph and concern themselves with most of the traditional questions of journalism: Who? What When? Where? How? Almost never does the Why? figure into these accounts, or even into much longer accounts, since this question is largely personal and understood as almost impossible to articulate anyway by most of the presumed audience. Joseph Conrad wrote of his novel *Chance:* "No doubt that by selecting a certain method and taking great pains the whole story might have been written out on a cigarette paper." He was responding to critics who complained about the length of his works. *American Alpine Journal* trip reports could be written on a cigarette paper.

The piece titled "Short Walks with McInerney: Three Classic Pilgrimages" contains the least literarily ambitious of the pieces collected here: they are straightforward telling for the most part.

As it turns out, the Mount Kennedy trip has commanded an inordinate amount of space in my own memory and thus reappears in a number of essays, like a Magic 8 Ball that, when consulted, reveals the same fortune over and over: not "It is certain," or "Reply hazy, try again," but "Mount Kennedy, Mount Kennedy, Mount Kennedy."

I understand completely David Roberts's repeated recounting of his climb and tragedy of Mount Huntington in the Alaska Range in 1965. The book *Mountain of My Fear,* which launched his career, was written eight months after the climb, when he was twenty-two years old, "in a white heat, a chapter a day, too impatient for second thoughts or serious revision." He also published four different accounts of the climb. And when he wrote his memoir *On the Ridge between Life and Death: A Climbing Life Re-examined* (2005), the Huntington trip appeared again. How could it not? As Roberts said of the climb, "I have never lived through a five-day span of comparable intensity." Such intensity occupies much more than five days' worth of memory.

I present these observations to defend the fact that in these essays, events and people reappear. Jorge Luis Borges said that the really great metaphors are always the same: "You compare time to a road, death to sleeping, life to dreaming. Those are the great metaphors because they respond to something essential." My memories are not metaphors, but they are like them in their essentiality.

If I didn't set out to write these essays as a book, I did at least set out to write, just as I set out to climb. For many years climbing came more easily to me with its insistence on focus, its engagement of the senses, its immersion in the natural world. Prufrock measured out his life in coffee spoon; Terry Tempest Williams measured hers in birds, at least she did during the time recounted in *Refuge*; for me it's mountains.

The challenges of the blank page were harder for me to commit to, a longer, slower road. Nonetheless, I have tried to adhere to Thoreau's dictum: "If one advances confidently in the direction of his dreams, and endeavors to live the life which he has imagined, he will meet with a success unexpected in the common hours."

I don't know about "confidently," and as far as "success" goes, all I know is that I continue to climb, and write, all in the direction of my dreams.

DDS
Anchorage, Alaska
September 2015

WARNINGS

AGAINST

MYSELF

In those early years, because of where we lived, climbing areas could be reached only by epic driving. We were Detroit's children, growing up in the flat shadows of industry. And so, being young, we once drove nonstop, three days and nights, five of us in a Plymouth Duster, to Mexico City. Twenty years ago, the air was not nearly so polluted as now, and driving through the city, I remember seeing great white clouds above us and to the east. It was my first experience of my favorite illusion: the mistaking of high, snow-covered mountains for clouds. When we realized they were the very mountains we had come so far to climb, we were exhilarated—children at Christmas—and we drove on through the village of Amecameca and up to Tlamacas, nestled between the great volcanoes Iztaccíhuatl and Popocatépetl.

We must have known about pulmonary edema and hypothermia, but we couldn't have known much, and as on many early climbs, we were lucky to have survived. At the time, of course, we thought that we had succeeded through determination, conditioning, skills learned from books, and our great desire. Now I think yes, about half those things, and half luck (luck especially in that no skill was required).

We spent the night in an odd building of roughly hewn stone. The sleeping area was more like a stable, or maybe a medieval brothel, with straw mats and fleas. We chose instead to sleep on the cement floors of a larger community room, watched over by a shrine to the Virgin of Guadalupe, before which departing climbers lit votive candles and made the sign of the cross.

Some climbers from Colorado were present, and, having succeeded on Popo, we were included in their conversation—a rich, satisfying feeling, as if our climb had purchased membership into an exclusive club. I remember few of the particulars of the conversations. We were talking about people, climbers, I remember that much. Doubtless I had nothing to say, the only climbers I knew being present in the room. Probably I was wondering if the scabs the sun had made of my lips, nose, and ears would ever go away. Or worrying whether there would be a graceful way to bail out of the next climb, Iztaccíhuatl.

The Coloradans were warning us to stay away from a certain person, a climber who was unsafe. They were vague, and we became curious. Was he here, this climber we were to avoid? No. Well, why then should we take care to avoid him? We might meet him someday—it's a small world, the worldly-wise Coloradans assured us. I remember thinking: *an unsafe climber*. I didn't really even know what sorts of sloppiness might cause someone to be labeled unsafe. I was thinking they might have meant "unlucky," in that bad accidents had happened to his partners (in which case it was they who were unlucky; he was lucky and resented for it). I had been reading Joseph Conrad's *Heart of Darkness* for the first time, and as the Coloradans were saying "unlucky," I kept hearing "unsound," as in the "unsound methods" of Kurtz.

How would we know this person? we asked. By his name, they said: David Stevenson.

I was floored by the trouble these guys had gone to in order to set me up—I didn't even know they knew my name. They assured me that they did not know my name, that the name of the unsafe climber was David Stevenson. I soon realized this was not an elaborate joke, but that, as they insisted, another climber out there in the world had my name. An unsafe climber. A person to be avoided at all costs.

I knew then it would be doubly hard to make a name for myself, hardly daring to admit to myself that this was what I intended. I thought of this shadowy other David Stevenson in those early years as I learned to climb—doubling up on anchors at belay points, backing up knots, checking my partner's harness. I wonder still what were the unspoken crimes of the other David Stevenson, if he is still alive, if he still climbs. This will be my twentieth year of climbing. I have been all over the United States and the world. It is odd, people say, that I have never climbed in Colorado. It is odd, I agree, just an accident of time and space, a small coincidence.

Although I think of my father as essentially pragmatic, we were a religious family. At my grandmother's was a book called *Lives of the Saints.* The saints were listed in order of their feast days—whether the days of their births or deaths, I was never quite sure. My favorite was Saint Sebastian because of the illustration of his martyrdom: he was tied to a tree, pierced with arrows, bleeding and haloed. Each time we visited I looked through that book to see if between visits an entry had miraculously appeared under my birthdate, if the pages had previously stuck together, or I had otherwise missed something. But I knew better. The free calendars that the ushers at church handed out on New Year's Day verified that no saints were celebrated on my birthday—it remained a blank square on the calendar.

As with seeing our names in print, when we read the date of our birth an inner alarm is set off, our interest heightened. We connect with the accompanying information in a personal, private way.

I was once reading one of the famous early accounts of climbing Everest, trying to picture the scene as clearly as possible, connecting time to distance between camps, calculating days at altitude. I realized that George Mallory and Andrew Irvine disappeared into the heights, and possibly reached the summit, on my birthday. They vanished nearly thirty years before I was born, so in my private rationalization of reincarnation and destiny, I account for this gap with a hazy sort of limbo. But then I remind myself that Tenzing Norgay and Edmund Hillary's summit ascent on May 29, 1953, was only a few days before my birth.

Such was my desperation to know my "destiny," to mystically connect myself to enterprises and achievements that I've come to value. So far I've managed to stay away from Everest, but even that is mostly chance—chance and finances. Not that one climbs Everest by chance—or does one? You have to do these things by design, of course, but not always by your own design: a friend or friend of a friend may initiate the idea, or you may be in the right place at the right time. Chance, maybe. We ride the coattails of our friends' dreams and they ours.

Given a choice, I would prefer to spend my birthday climbing, but I'm usually working. I have spent most of my life as a student or a teacher, and my birthday invariably falls in the last week of the semester, when my workload is heaviest. I usually plan a long, hard run to compare with birthday runs of years past to tell me how old I really am. The one birthday I spent climbing was memorable, a single day in the middle of a thirty-five-day expedition.

We were on Mount Kennedy in the St. Elias Range near the Alaska-Yukon border, descending from high camp to base camp—about three thousand feet of rappelling. The weather was okay—that is, not a factor. But I remember being incredibly tired even as we started. I hadn't slept much in the three nights at high camp, four of us in a two-person tent with only two sleeping bags. The platform we had chopped out of the ice was not quite large enough for the base of the tent, so one side hung over the edge, and the first night there, the way I recall it, I remained roped up inside the tent. We ran out of food, fuel, energy, and good weather before I got a chance to try for the summit, but a couple of guys made it, and getting them there was a team effort.

The descent was taking forever. We had some very long ropes, enabling us to do rappels of up to three hundred feet (about twice the length of a normal pitch), but it was still taking a long time. We had a system: at the end of a rappel we would clip ourselves into an anchor and then clip our packs into the anchor so we could take them off to set up the next rap.

We were descending, as we had climbed, in pairs: Jack and Scott, Alan and myself. On the long rappels Alan and I, out in front, were quite alone. We had begun in marginal weather, descending into the clouds. By this time we had been up and down enough times stocking high camp that routefinding was no problem, but when it snowed, the route became a natural funnel for small spindrift avalanches or, if it snowed for long, larger avalanches (while we were there, it once snowed nonstop for seven days). So even though there was good reason to get down off the route, there was no point in hurrying with so far to go. The last thousand feet were particularly familiar to us, Alan and I having been that far at least twice before. I relaxed mentally.

Alan was below and out of sight as the rope cut diagonally across a rocky face. I clipped myself into the anchor, clipped my pack in, and disconnected my descender, a cast aluminum figure eight, from the rope. As the figure eight melted itself into the snow, hot from the friction of the rope, I estimated rope lengths to the glacier, wondering if base camp looked larger than it had from the last anchor or if this were only wishful thinking. The weather had cleared, and the sun was casting mountainous shadows across the Kennedy Glacier. My pack shifted on its sling, slid a few feet and was airborne. It bounced twice, spinning wildly. I watched, stunned that the carabiner hadn't closed, checking the 'biner that held me to the anchor, and feeling suddenly very lucky, the sound of my heart beating loudly in my ears.

I was called back to the world by Alan shouting my name, and realized that the pack, with several hundred feet of rope and a five-gallon fuel container lashed to it, was a massive, human-shaped thing, and that to Alan, a couple hundred feet away, it was me that appeared to be spinning toward the glacier. When I reached him, Alan said, "I thought..."

"I know," I said.

Hours later, when we got down to where the climb had begun, I could see my pack, still a hundred yards below us on the glacier, hardly damaged, its contents strewn about. Alan and I began digging for our skis, which we had planted tails down at the base of the climb, and which now, only a few days later, were buried under several feet of snow. We were still digging when Jack and Scott arrived, and it took us hours more to find the skis. I collected my pack, Alan noting that he would have gladly launched his, if only he had known it wouldn't completely blow apart. Then we skied the three or four hundred yards back to base camp, where Terrible Terry Boley had been brewing up tea and dinner. Skiing those last yards to camp I remember as a great, blissful relief—we were (or so we felt) out of danger, out from underneath the pressure we had put on ourselves to reach the summit.

Someone took a photograph of me, then, before we reached camp. It shows me exhausted, wind- and sunburned, the stuff of my pack tied on just well enough to hold for a quarter mile. At base camp we were reunited with Terrible, who had manned camp alone for six days. Occasionally we had seen him skiing across the glacier, throwing a long shadow across the snow. From our great height we could sometimes see the shadows of snowed-in crevasses that he unknowingly skied over; but most of the time we couldn't see down (or up either) because of the weather, and when we could, Terry's movements at camp weren't distinguishable from the tent and supplies.

Despite our exhaustion, we were exhilarated to be down. It was like a family reunion: as if base camp were home, Terry the patriarch of our family, and our days on the mountain a prodigal outing on which we had squandered our resources and from which we had returned utterly spent. Terrible took us in and melted pot after pot of snow, and we drank tea with milk and sugar until early the next morning.

We asked him what he had done in the days he had spent alone. The question caught him completely off guard, as if we had demanded an impromptu explanation of quantum physics. "I don't know," he said. We laughed at this; we laughed at everything. (Later, when we were home, we saw an roll of exquisite infrared photographs Terrible had shot—an eerie testimony to his lost days.) At some time in the night I remembered it was my birthday, and I became even happier to be alive to reach the grand age of twenty-four. I figured I knew things about myself unknown to me five weeks before, though what those things were I would have been hard pressed to articulate. I felt like F. Scott Fitzgerald's Nick Carraway, suddenly remembering his thirtieth birthday in the twilight of a day filled with love and death. Nick saw before him "the portentous menacing road of a new decade." But I felt I had put some vaguely menacing thing behind me, and ahead I saw a life, a reprieve maybe, taking shape out of experience, as one day Terrible's photographs of his lost days would assume their surprising shapes in the developing trays.

Hearing the news about Dave Kahn was like a scene out of fiction or a movie. The phone rang unexpectedly, late—static on the line, long distance. "Have you heard about Kahn?" the voice asked.

"No," I said, not quite sure who was on the line.

"Dead," he said.

The caller hadn't known how much I liked Kahn, what good friends we had been. The summer we worked together at Early Winters, neither of us was climbing much. I had returned worn out and climbed out from an expedition; Kahn was in the midst of a series of shoulder operations that he hoped would leave him able to climb to his full potential. I thought of him as a climbing partner, but in actuality we never climbed together.

Kahn was an equipment freak: I still have a perfectly good down sleeping bag I bought from him when he replaced it with something newer. When the self-taught perfectionist Mike Schonhofen was designing backpacks, he used to hide from Kahn, who always had new, idiosyncratic modifications to suggest. About Kahn's shoulder operations, Schonhofen claimed, "He finally got tired of customizing his equipment; now he's into customizing his own body."

After the summer we worked together, I saw Kahn only two more times, once at Bill Edwards's wedding, where we drank excellent champagne. Bill was one of the partners at Early Winters, an equipment designer and very competent ice climber. The only photograph I have of Dave was taken at the wedding, a clear shot. Although his face is in the shade, he's looking at me behind the lens, as if, in fact, it were Kahn making the photograph. The last time I saw Kahn was at the outdoor equipment trade show in Las Vegas, where the industry conducts its yearly business. It's a sort of gathering of the tribes; my attendance was purely social.

I had heard Kahn was in town and had left a message for him. I was sleeping on Schonhofen's hotel room floor. Kahn showed up late, after I was asleep, or passed out: we were, after all, in Las Vegas. Neither of us wanted to drink anymore, so we ended up walking around the golf course at the Sands, talking most of the night.

Kahn was surprised with his own success: the company he worked for was in the midst of a meteoric rise (later it would crash just as quickly). They were sending him to Europe, to some huge sporting-goods show in Germany. His own good fortune amazed him: he was doing exactly what he wanted to do, and climbing too. He was planning to climb in the Alps and wanted to know what I had done over there.

My climbing during my summer in Europe was all moderate stuff. I had done one climb with a fierce reputation, but the conditions were so perfect that it had gone quickly, most of it before the sun rose, before I could actually grasp the dizzying verticality of the thing. He wanted to know what I would do if I went back. He was beginning to make plans, jotting down a few notes on the backs of business cards. He wanted to know about Chamonix.

I told him about the Dru. I told him about planning to climb it with this Mexican guy I met, how we had arranged to meet, go up and give the American Direct a look. The American Direct on the

Dru is uncharacteristic of the routes above Chamonix. It's all rock, no ice or snow, and it happened to have been climbed first by Americans. Perhaps Javier thought that by doing the route with an actual American he would be charmed, his success assured.

That night I had one of those climbing nightmares: even if you've never climbed, you know the one. You wake up in a cold sweat knowing that you are about to fall, frozen in that interminable moment before you actually come off. In the dream I was most definitely on the Dru. I woke clear-headed, knowing I wasn't sharp enough on rock to handle the difficulties and commitment of that climb. So I went down to the train station to meet Javier and tell him. I was in street clothes, not carrying a pack, feeling like a tourist. I felt such sweet relief. There at the station was Javier, also in street clothes. We laughed, walked back up to the avenue Michel Croz, and ordered up brandy with our coffee. "How do you say in *ingles*?" Javier wanted to know. "Chickenshit," I told him, and we laughed like madmen.

I told Kahn I'd like to be in good enough shape to do the Dru next time I went back. "The American Direct," I said, "Oh yeah, definitely, the Dru." That was the last time I saw Kahn.

On the phone I wanted details. "Dead how?"

"No one knows, except that he was climbing and he fell."

"Come on, you've got to know more. Fell how?"

"No one knows. I just heard today. Apparently it was like two months ago. He was on the Dru and he fell and he's dead. That's all anyone knows."

I was trying to imagine all the scenarios—rockfall? weather? Was he with a partner? Was he unroped? I have never talked to anyone who knew the answers. The caller said that before he left for Europe, Kahn had changed, that he was somehow promoting himself as a big-time alpinist, as a guide, that he had lost his sense of perspective. I wouldn't know about that. I do know that even though we didn't run into each other much, I liked the idea of Kahn being out there in the world. I don't think of myself as superstitious, but I couldn't help feeling that maybe Dave Kahn caught the bullet I'd dodged. I haven't been back to Chamonix since then.

Although I own many, many books about climbing, I never owned a copy of *Accidents in North American Mountaineering* until a well-meaning acquaintance picked an old one, from 1965, out of a box of books at an estate sale. I suppose I thought these annual volumes were meant for search-and-rescue types, or that interest in them was indecorous, somehow prurient, or maybe just the fear that contemplation of such things becomes self-fulfilling prophecy. Thumbing through its pages, the first account I focused on is told by David A. Stevenson (I am a David D. Stevenson). This Stevenson relates an accident involving a failed ice-axe belay on Sharkfin Tower in the North Cascades. I know the place, the trail you turn off to get there. The victim was Stevenson's wife, Fran, who suffered a fractured neck. I asked my wife what she thought of this. "What a coincidence," she said. "You have a dog named Fran." I did not think this was the same person as the Coloradan David Stevenson I had been warned against, Colorado and Washington being somehow mutually exclusive in those days.

For a while, years ago, my wife told me I ought to try to use my middle name, Dougal, when I sent writing out for publication. I had to explain that I couldn't do that because people might think me pretentious, as my middle name is the first name of a famous climber. She thought my father was the only other Dougal in the world. I told her about Dougal Haston.

I worshipped Haston and Doug Scott in those days. I had just arrived in Seattle when Doug Scott came to town on a lecture tour, showing his slides of the southwest face of Everest. There was a terrifying photograph that pictured two box tents pitched on what looked to be a near-vertical snowfield; it was beyond the powers of my imagination. The magnitude of what they had done overwhelmed me. Later in Chris Bonington's *Everest the Hard Way*, the captions for the photographs became iconic to me:

"Dougal Haston climbing the Hillary Step."

"Dougal just above the Hillary Step. Lhotse and Nuptse Ridge in the middle distance."

"Haston leading through towards the final slope of the summit, the Chinese emblem just visible."

In those days I climbed almost every weekend with Roy, who did virtually all the leading and who taught me a lot. Our friendship was sealed after we discovered that we lived in nearly identical slum apartments on opposite sides of Seattle. We competed to see who could live the most Spartan existence. Roy pounded the red plastic off his Swiss Army knife and hacksawed off the unnecessary blades to save weight on climbs. He called me "Dolomite" after the hopelessly clunky klettershoes I wore. I didn't think they held me back too much, except on smooth slabs. We climbed mostly at Peshastin Pinnacles or on Snow Creek Wall. Peshastin had its own scene: even back then you often had to wait in line for the popular routes, and there were always people watching. Once Roy was about fifteen feet off the ground when he became very conscious of his audience. He began yelling down to me, calling me "Gaston," babbling away, narrating his own progress—but in French, which was news to me. We were more Cro-Magnon than French and struggled even with our native tongue. As I belayed, people asked, "Where're you from, man?" To which I shrugged idiotically, unable to fake a single phrase, but not willing to admit my partner was a lunatic. Of course they assumed I knew no English. "They're from Europe," some guy said. "Check out the shoes."

I received a phone call at work—it had to have been at work as I didn't have a telephone at my apartment. Roy worked in a hightech tent factory; he spoke in low tones. "They're here. Can you get away?" he asked.

"Who?"

"Haston and Scott," he whispered. "They're here."

They were on their way to Mount McKinley (Denali), where they ended up doing a new route on the upper south face. But I couldn't get away from work, so I begged Roy to stay on the phone and re-port the details of the royal visit. Haston and Scott were just hang-ing out, spending as much time as was polite if they were going to walk out with a free tent to "test" on McKinley. According to Roy, Haston didn't say much, didn't seem to be as comfortable among strangers as Scott. Haston was quiet, serious, perhaps already look-ing ahead to McKinley—it's hard to imagine they could have been worried about it. The Everest climb had been just the year before. He looked, Roy reported, exactly like the photograph in Boning-ton's book.

Months later, an avalanche buried Dougal Haston. He was ski touring near Leysin, Switzerland, "minutes from his home." Ac-counts I read described the accident in just those words, made to sound pedestrian against the grandeur of his career on the cutting edge. The climbing world mourned its loss, and I shared their aston-ishment and emptiness, felt it personally.

When I was in the Midwest last summer, I saw one of my oldest friends, Mick DeGiulio. Such a rendezvous was sheer luck, as he too lives far from where we grew up. We managed to find time for a long, fast run together. Afterwards, when we were reliving the old days, Mick said, "Remember when you used to say you thought you would die young, like before thirty?" I couldn't remember ever saying that or thinking that. But his question stayed with me, and finally I admitted to myself that I had once been that person Mick re-membered. Maybe it was an adopted romantic pose, or more likely that I simply could not foresee my future.

In the course of a year I'd had two frightening experiences in the mountains. They actually occurred on consecutive New Year's Eves. The first was on another trip to Mexico. I was traveling by myself, meeting people to climb with here and there. This trip was to Iztac-cíhuatl, the beautiful "sleeping lady." The features of the mountain form the profile of a woman lying down, and its features are labeled from north to south: La Cabeza, the head, to Las Pies, the feet. I have never been one to attribute gender to the mountains, but here, at least, was a topographical reason.

Our chosen route on Iztaccíhuatl was the Directa al Pecho—that is, directly up the breast, the summit being El Pecho. We were a motley group. My main partner was a guy I had talked into the experience. A nonclimber, he had rented equipment from a Mexico City shop. His crampons and ice axe looked like quaint decorations you might find hanging above a condo fireplace in a resort town. The approach hike was long. It followed an ancient aqueduct system that created a belt of moisture, causing the vegetation to grow wildly and giving the hike the feel of high rain forest. Along the way we were joined by a couple of Mexican climbers and a Colombian who'd been to graduate school at U Mass, Amherst. It appeared I was the most experienced climber of the group, which wasn't saying much.

Our summit bid ended in a whiteout about an hour from the El Pecho hut when one of the Mexicans, Carlos, cartwheeled by us, looking like a cartoon character forming a human snowball. He did not use his ice axe to self-arrest, or even appear to grasp the concept. He passed within a few yards of me, and our eyes met in a split second out of time, a frozen frame in a loop of high-action film. He stopped a hundred or so yards down, where the slope leveled out. I remember descending to Carlos's body expecting the worst. I remember thinking that since we were descending facing the slope, it was probably steep enough that we should have been roped up. But if we had been roped up, probably we would all have been heaped together with Carlos in a bloody tangle. As luck would have it, Carlos was neither dead nor bloody. We retreated to the hut to consider our options and celebrate the new year; if the weather cleared, we could try the next day. We drank hot lemonade and tequila from a canteen that we passed around.

Later that night when the hallucinations began, I wasn't sure of the cause—the altitude (over sixteen thousand feet), food poisoning, or both. In my delirium, the forces of the universe conspired to keep me on the mountain. I was suffocating. I had to get away. I left the tent and wandered onto the glacier in my stocking-clad feet. Someone retrieved me and talked me back, leading me by the hand like a man talked down from a window ledge. In the morning I woke clear-headed—vomiting and with diarrhea, but no longer hallucinating. However, my feet were frozen. There was nothing to do but walk out.

I remember taking the bus to the hospital in Mexico City. At one of the bus stops the bus came to jerky halt, stopping, as it turned out, with one of its tires on the foot of a small child. After much shouting and wailing, the child's foot was freed, but flattened, and, conveniently for me, the driver drove him directly to the hospital, where I spent the night rehydrating with an IV stuck in my arm. I spent several weeks recovering in Cuernavaca. In the cool mornings I sat on the benches in the Jardín Borda, watching aspiring bullfighters learn their trade.

The next year found us trying to traverse New Hampshire's Presidential Range in midwinter. Although the peaks in this range do not rise much above six thousand feet, they are quite remote, especially in winter. And while the traverse itself requires no significant technical skills, the weather is severe: winds over two hundred miles per hour are not uncommon, and the average temperature in winter hovers just above zero Fahrenheit. There were three of us, friends from high school, and McInerney had failed to make the traverse on three previous attempts. The one time I had been with him, we hiked the first six miles congratulating ourselves for having the good sense to have left suburban Detroit and patting ourselves on the back for being so cool, the evidence for which was the fact that there we were undertaking such a worthy and glorious enterprise. That night it was so cold we were afraid to go to sleep. The morning dawned bright and clear, but, already beaten, we turned back.

This time we started in the middle of the night because of a favorable weather forecast. The whole enterprise was a gamble with the weather. On our second night we had made so much progress that our third guy, McDonnell, who had not been on the earlier failures, declared that he felt we were somehow cheating because we had not been "challenged by the weather." On hearing this, McInerney and I knew immediately that we were doomed.

The next morning the wind blew up, and the air thickened with clouds. We were literally crawling on all fours when a gust of wind blew a hole in the white. The Lakes of the Clouds Hut appeared momentarily not thirty feet from us—otherwise we might never have found it. We spent two or three nights there, one of which was New Year's Eve. We stumbled out to the highway after two days of wading through waist-deep snow in corduroy knickers. McDonnell was incoherent with hypothermia, and we tormented him for years afterward for the curse he had brought down on us. He never climbed again—after becoming a surgeon, he claimed he couldn't risk injuring his fingers.

By the next year I had moved west. When New Year's Eve rolled around, I had no particular reason to be in the mountains, because I was in the mountains all the time: my climbing no longer required vacation time or travel. I remember being at a party thinking about the two previous New Year's Eves. In an advanced state of drunkenness, we went to a Chinese restaurant. My fortune cookie read: "You shall gain your wish." I was sobered and humbled by that reminder of my general state of confusion: I did not even know my own wish. I felt unprepared for my good fortune.

So when I put DeGiulio's memory of me into perspective, it fits, embarrassing though it is. Luck had something to do with my surviving those early climbs, and the future was shrouded in uncertainty. How could I have then guessed what fortune might be holding for me?

There was a time in my youth, the limbo between adolescence and adulthood, when my father and I didn't communicate so clearly. I could hardly expect him to understand what I was doing when I didn't know myself. Once, when I was home from college for the weekend, he looked at my longish hair and early beard and said,

"Look at you. You don't even look like yourself." I did not then know how a person could look like anyone other than himself.

Our strategy on Mount Kennedy was for the four of us to work together to establish a high camp, and then for Alan and me to return to base camp and bring up more food and fuel so we could wait out the weather for a summit attempt. The plan was accomplished, up to a point. However, when Alan and I were back at base, I found myself so shaken by the unrelenting exposure that I was paralyzed with vertigo. I vowed never to return to high camp, that the wavering and unknowable line between sanity and insanity had for once been clearly and fixedly revealed to me. Moments later, Alan discovered the tent poles in his pack, meaning we had returned from high camp and left Jack and Scott up there without a tent. At about the same time it began snowing, and the snow would continue for seven days.

On the second day, Jack appeared out of the whiteout to retrieve the poles. He looked like the sparrows that occasionally fluttered into camp to eat out of our hands. Sometimes we would find them frozen in a hollow space just below the surface of the glacier. We watched in amazement the next day when Jack set out again for high camp, the thundering of avalanches echoing in the invisible amphitheater above.

Later, at base camp, someone suggested that we should just smoke up the rest of the dope and ski on out the seventy-five miles to the highway, where we could get a cheeseburger—that we'd seen the last of them.

When the weather cleared, we could hear some yelling from above, but it was unintelligible. When Alan and I reached high camp, Scott and Jack were nearly out of food and fuel, but they were well. The position of the tent appeared no more hospitable than it had earlier. Even stepping out of it seemed an unnecessary risk: we pissed into a canteen (later marked with a skull and crossbones). Scott looked to me like a physically different person, hollow-cheeked and ashen-faced. I was convinced that his hair had grayed in the course of seven nights. I didn't think I should mention it at the time.

Much later, on the way out, I said to Scott, "You don't even look like the same person. Your hair's gray!" Scott took this as a criticism, I think, and said, "Take a look in the mirror, pal. You don't look so good yourself." I was completely exhausted. We didn't know how many days we were from the road; we didn't know if we could get across the Kaskawalsh, a huge Alaskan river swollen by spring rains and glacier melt. We didn't know if our food would last. My nose started bleeding for about the tenth time. I lay on top of my pack with my head tilted back to stop the bleeding. We didn't have any mirrors on the trip, but someone snapped a picture of me at that moment: later I would see that Scott was right.

Once as I was leaving my parents' home to return west, my father said to wait a minute, he had something for me. I could not imagine what it might be: my father's best gifts were never material things. He brought out a pair of black silk gloves. He figured they might be useful for some kind of climbing-related activity, like tying knots in the cold. I held the gloves in my hands; indeed, they looked like they might be useful for just that.

"Where'd you get them?" I asked.

"They gave them to us when I was a pallbearer at this funeral," he said.

"Oh," I said, wondering if this were some kind of joke. I asked who died, and he told me it was the father of someone at work. A good friend? I asked. No, he said, a guy he barely knew. I thanked my father, listening in my voice for betrayal of the awkwardness that accompanies a thoughtful but useless gift. Wearing the gloves climbing was unimaginable; in truth, wearing them at all was unimaginable. I still have them, faded with years, though they have never seen the light of day. My father is a man utterly without superstition.

1990

This essay was written twenty-five years ago, when I was living in Salt Lake City and working on a graduate degree in English. Most of the climbing recounted here took place in the mid-1970s. Some of the statements I made then—"I have never climbed in Colorado," for example—are no longer true. My grandmother's book *Lives of the Saints* now sits on my shelf, years after her passing. And while it was possible twenty-five years ago to believe that Mallory and Irvine might have summited Everest, in light of more recent discoveries it seems highly unlikely today.

Many of us still mourn the early death of Dave Kahn on the Dru, including Bill Edwards and Mark Twight, with whom I have spoken fondly of Dave in the last year. Mark sent a photo of Dave's marker in the Chamonix cemetery.

Finally, I noticed a huge exaggeration in the original published version of this essay, which I have amended here—and I am relieved to say this is the only essay in the book that required such a change. In the original, I placed myself in the room with Haston and Scott at Early Winters. In reality, as I state here, I couldn't get away from work and had to settle for Roy narrating the visit for me over the telephone. That earlier exaggeration is embarrassing, and I am glad to be able to set the record straight here. In any case, my interest in Haston has persisted: see the recent essay "Whillans, Haston, and Me" in these pages.

My father passed away in 2012. He remained without superstition to the end of his days.

SPEAKING
IN CODE

Conversations and Reflections on Climbing,

Language, and the Religion of the French

In every game is contained the idea of death.

—Jim Morrison

ON PRACTICE CLIMBING

When I first arrived in the West, I was broke and working all the time. I didn't have any climbing partners, and there was no money for gas. Those first months I took comfort from just knowing the mountains were there: in Seattle, that was sometimes a matter of faith. On clear days I was a kid with a happy secret, just from being able to see Rainier and the Olympic Range. A guy I worked with told me about a place to do practice climbs.

"Practice climbs?" I didn't know what he meant.

"Yeah, you know, short climbs. Not on real mountains."

The place he was talking about was called Snow Creek Wall, across Stevens Pass, near Leavenworth. The first practice climb I did there turned out to be a grade III. In those days few climbs were short enough that I couldn't turn them into an epic. My friend Roy led every hard pitch, and we topped off in the dark, exhausted and dehydrated. On the descents we thrashed through the brush and blindly rappelled off trees toward the sound of Snow Creek.

Later that season, Roy did a practice climb with someone else on Snow Creek Wall. They got caught in a July snowstorm and had to bivy without overnight gear. That route was a grade IV. Practice for what? That's what I was wondering, half a season of climbing in the West under my belt.

CLIMBING

Someone has written about the early days of climbing when, if you saw a pair of lug-soled footprints in the mountains, chances were good they belonged to someone you knew. It wasn't quite like that when I began climbing, but sometimes it felt like that.

Some of us decided we would try to do a first winter ascent of Liberty Ridge on Mount Rainier. We were very organized and kept our packs loaded with food and fuel, ready for some kind of break in the weather. As it happened, the weather turned very bad before we got too high up, which was probably just as well because there were five of us, all equally less experienced than we thought ourselves to be, and, in hindsight, it seems clear that something worse would have happened had we gone on.

At our high point, we were camped in a heavily crevassed area somewhere near where the Carbon Glacier meets the base of Liberty Ridge. Visibility was about twenty feet, and the wind kept picking up the tent and slamming it down. All five of us were in the one tent, lying down more or less on top of each other, because the hooped poles were being flattened by the winds. We debated about what to do as if there were really a choice to be made. No one wanted to say he was definitely for going down, the sooner the better. To do anything else would have been lunacy, but those were the days when macho lunacy often prevailed over common sense: we were lucky to have lived through that time.

Even with all five of us in there, the wind kept picking us up and slamming us down, picking us up and slamming us down. There may have been some praying. That was about the time Bill Edwards went into his "backpacking trance." He began in dreamy, faraway voice. "Dave," he said, "have you ever been backpacking?" He asked it like backpacking was something he would very much like to do again, should he survive the night. I knew he meant backpacking as an end in itself, not on the way to a climb. Actually, I never had done that. Then he talked about backpacking in the Sierra. He made it sound like the Garden of Eden. He described high traverses through alpine terrain, endless blue skies, and nightly panfuls of freshly caught and fried lake trout. (Years later I would find out that his description was fairly accurate.) Bill was a heckuva ice climber, but I don't remember him climbing too much after that.

On the way out the weather cleared somewhat. Down below the snowline we met a couple parties on their way to try routes on the Willis Wall, also on the north side of Rainier, which, like Liberty Ridge, had seen no recorded winter ascents. In one group were Scott Baker and Jack Lewis, with whom I would later become great friends and who were my companions on my finest days in the mountains, a second ascent of the north ridge of Mount Kennedy in the St. Elias Range—a thirty-five-day trip with an approach on skis. The other pair of climbers was Al Givler and Dusan Jagersky, well-known Seattle climbers who were older than us and more seasoned alpinists by far. The good weather held for them, and both groups were successful. Their success led us to rationalizing that only the weather had kept us from completing our climb, but, like I said, that doesn't even seem remotely likely now.

After the St. Elias trip the next year, I returned to Seattle by ferry from Haines, Alaska. The Inside Passage was a hazy idyll, the scenery rolling slowly by us like a gigantic Chinese mural. We slept on deck with about nine cents in our pockets, confusing the exhilaration of being alive with a kind of immortality. Aisha, my girlfriend (now my wife), met me at the dock. She was especially glad to see me because two climbers had just been reported killed in Alaska, and their names hadn't yet been made known. The article was in that morning's *Seattle Times*. It was Al and Dusan. They had slipped while descending an unnamed peak in the Fairweather Range. I burst into tears. I didn't even know where the Fairweather Range was.

ON THE UNION WALL

At the university where I teach, I spend as much time as I can in one building. When my day goes as planned, I leave the building only to get coffee, surprisingly good coffee, at the student union. A corner of the union is built with large blocks of stone that now bear the chalk marks of climbers. It's a good-sized wall, maybe fifteen feet high and twenty feet across; it turns a corner and follows a set of stairs. I've never climbed on it or on any other buildings, though I admit that for years I've looked at buildings as potential climbs, surreptitiously testing edges close to the ground.

These days, more often than not, there are climbers on the union wall. One day my wife and some friends met me at my office. As we walked over to the union for coffee, we saw the climbers—Lycra-clad, white-palmed, sweaty shoulders bared.

"That's disgusting," Aisha said. In general, although she doesn't come right out and admit it, my wife is less than enthusiastic about my climbing. Friends and relatives of hers have died climbing; some of them had children. When she says, "That's disgusting," I hear more: "Because it's so ostentatious." But someone we're walking with doesn't know our code; they want to know why it's disgusting.

"Well," Aisha says, "It's like having sex with an inflatable doll." I'm wondering what she's been reading, but I think I know what she means. Our friends are looking at her as if to say, "Yikes! Maybe she shouldn't have any more coffee." Sensing this, she adds, "In public," as if now the connection will be obvious to all. "Yes," she repeats. "Sex with an inflatable doll in public."

It's a fair enough analogy, I decide. Nonetheless, I feel compelled to defend the climbers. "It's a good pump," I shrug. *Pump* is not a word I would normally use in this context, in this company. I explain that by *pump* I mean roughly "exhausting workout." "No sexual innuendo intended," I add, "unlike your crude analogy."

"Why can't they just do pull-ups in the privacy of their own basements like normal people?"

"It's not the same," I say.

"Exactly," she says.

ON LEADING

Whenever we bouldered at Rubidoux, in Southern California, we would end the day by traversing on a man-made wall on the east side of the mountain overlooking Riverside. Usually it was evening, and it was good to be out of the sun. We'd go back and forth, never more than a few inches above the ground. The idea was to get make your forearms burn just enough that by the time you hit the car you could just barely grip the steering wheel. The wall follows a baked-dirt road, and a little stone bridge that connects nothing to nothing goes over the road and connects to the wall. Climbers would climb the inside wall of the bridge and go as far as they could along the top of the arch, dropping off onto the road, careful their feet came off first so they didn't land on their backs.

One night we were standing around debating whether we had a few more laps in us or if it was time to head down to the Mexican restaurant visible just below us, across from the cemetery. Then we saw a curious sight: a cloud of dust coming straight toward us, uphill through the brush. The trails that lead to the bouldering on Rubidoux rise a few hundred yards from the valley floor and switch back a couple times. But this was coming straight for us—*direttissima*. At first it appeared to be a mightily determined dog, but soon a human shape emerged, moving, for some reason, on all fours. We watched until finally the guy popped over the edge of the slope onto the road. He was young, covered in dust, and streaked with sweat. His muscles rippled and twitched, and he breathed hard. He stood there silent except for the panting, like a hunting dog after the chase, maybe even with a hint of foam about the mouth. Climbing shoes were tied to his belt loops. He was a healthy young animal, and when he collected his breath we were talking climbing. He was referring to the routes here by numbers—22, 23. For a second I thought he might be using the Australian rating system, that he didn't know about 5.10 or 5.11. It turned out he only knew the difficulty of routes according to the numbers they were assigned in a competition. Not only was he not a part of the larger climbing world, he wasn't even aware of such a world. It was as if he didn't exist at all outside Rubidoux.

So far as we could tell, he had mastered nearly all the classic local problems any of us knew about. "Have you done much at Joshua Tree or Tahquitz?" someone asked.

"Where are they?"

His ignorance was inconceivable to those of us standing around. These places are scarcely more than an hour's drive from Rubidoux, and climbers from all over the world travel to them. We looked at each other in mild exasperation.

"You should try leading," one of us offered.

"Leading?" I can't say that he actually mispronounced it, but he said it blankly, like you'd say an unknown word in a foreign language—only a sound, empty and without meaning.

ON SPORT CLIMBING

The term refers to routes that are protected by bolts, usually preset by a first ascent party. It is a far less risky enterprise than traditional climbing, in which each party is responsible for placing his or her own protection. What I like about the term *sport climbing* is that, by implication, it suggests that the rest of climbing is something other than sport. I have always preferred to think that climbing transcends categories like sport, games, and especially, recreation.

I don't think climbing is much like bullfighting either, although Hemingway has a character in *The Sun Also Rises* who responds as some might to climbing. On hearing of a matador gored to death in the ring, a waiter is disgusted. "All for sport," he says. "All for pleasure." He hated bullfighting, of course, but he may just as well have been redefining *sport* and *pleasure*. We do the same most of the time when we apply those words to climbing.

Sport climbing may be a more apt description. In a couple different pieces of recent fiction I have encountered the term *sportfucking*. (I imagine my wife reading over my shoulder as I type, asking, "What have you been reading?") From the contexts, the meaning of *sportfucking* is clear: athletic sex, no love, no commitment. So what is sport climbing exactly? How is it like other types of climbing? More importantly, how is it different? What exactly does it mean to fix the adjective or prefix *sport* to a word?

ON 5.13

I found out quite by accident that an acquaintance of mine, a guy I play basketball with, is a climber. He had just started the previous season but had gotten out all the time, he said. The climbing is close to where we live; you can make a lot of progress in a year. He asked me how long I had been climbing. Well, I have been climbing a long time, and I felt that to actually say the number of years would sound arrogant, so I shrugged casually, "Oh, quite a while."

"Well, how hard is the stuff you climb?"

He caught me off guard there. I had always thought that was a question to be danced around, or otherwise politely avoided, for as long as possible. I felt a bit embarrassed that he would ask: embarrassed for him, that is, like you would be for someone who, through no fault of their own, had never learned manners. So I answered as before, as casually as I could, "Oh, around 5.9 or 5.10, it depends."

I could see that somehow the answer embarrassed him; he looked away from my glance like my dog pretending not to hear me.

"So how long did you say you've been climbing?" Spoken as if it had somehow caused him pain to ask.

"Oh, seventeen, eighteen years." I knew exactly, but felt it more modest to be imprecise. I wasn't catching on at all.

He paused a second, then it was out. "So, what's the problem?"

Finally, I got it—he was embarrassed for me. I'd been climbing for all these years, and here I was still bumbling along at 5.10. He was serious: he wondered if I had stopped climbing for six or seven years, been in a car accident or something. If I really was a climber, and had been really climbing for all that time, it was inconceivable to him that I wasn't climbing 5.13. Something, he figured, was very, very wrong.

ON THE RELIGION OF THE FRENCH

Where we now live, many people are very religion-conscious. Once when Aisha was confronted with the rude question "What religion are you?" her friend came to her rescue with: "She's French, of course. Can't you see?" This was my wife's formal baptism into the religion she had been living for years. The religion of French, as practiced by my wife, consists mostly of drinking Chardonnay in the afternoon, smoking Gitanes Bout Filtres, listening to Edith Piaf, and seeing French films. Occasionally, she splurges on an exquisite (expensively so) fabric or dress with the rationale that such purchases are essential to her spiritual well-being. She can read French, too. She has sometimes helped me translate difficult passages in *Vertical* articles. Interestingly enough, though her French is excellent, it's of minimal help. She has to translate twice. Not only are the articles in French, but they are in the language of the mountains, a language equally foreign to her: *arête, bivouac, cirque, couloir, crevasse, massif, moraine, sérac.*

On the way to Snowbird for the World Cup International Sport Climbing Championships it is necessary to drive by Gate Buttress, probably the most popular rock climbing area in the Wasatch Mountains. We drove past at least two dozen routes that I knew to be excellent, which I had not yet done, and which I would like very much to do. At Snowbird we didn't have lawn chairs, but all I could think of was an old Galen Rowell photograph of a spectator watching big-wall climbers in Yosemite. In the picture, the man is comfortable in a down jacket and lawn chair, his spotting scope is mounted on a tripod and aimed upward. There was a time when I had a smug attitude about the person in that photograph.

Like just about everyone at Snowbird, Aisha and I (especially Aisha) were greatly impressed by Patrick Edlinger's performance. All the French—Didier Raboutou and Marc Le Menestrel particularly—climbed with a grace and sureness that was fun to watch. However, during the contest I continued to feel uneasy about my change in status from active participant to spectator. My wife pointed out that I had never participated in a climbing contest or climbed on the side of a building—that I was never a participant in this activity. She further pointed out that I spend a lot of time thinking, reading, and writing about climbing. These, she reminded me, are not exactly active pursuits. I had been thinking about the sameness of this and other types of climbing, when it is the differences that are most important. As a nonclimber, Aisha had a much fresher perspective. "Your hair," she noted, "is as long as Edlinger's. Almost the same color too." It wasn't necessary to add that the similarities ended there.

"Of course the French excel at this," she said later.

"Why is that?"

"It is the elevation of style over substance," she said, as if this were the final word on the subject.

It sounded like she might be right but I didn't know quite exactly what she meant. "It's your religion," I shrugged.

The French are on the cutting edge of language and literary theory, too. In fact, modern semiotics, the study of signs and symbols, was founded by Ferdinand de Saussure in 1916 with the publication of *Cours de linguistique generale* (Course in General Linguistics). The basis of his ideas is that signs—such as letters and words—have meaning because of their differences from other signs. Where it begins to get tricky is with his notion that language precedes the existence of the objects to which it refers; that the world is knowable only by differentiating between concepts. It is an interesting, and probably meaningless, coincidence that it was another Frenchman, another de Saussure (Horace-Bénédict), whose early ascent of Mont Blanc in 1787 helped to launch modern alpinism.

Today it is Jacques Derrida (and others of his compatriots—Roland Barthes, Michel Foucault, and Jacques Lacan, among them) who shake the foundations of linguistic scholarship. Derrida practices a kind of reading called deconstruction. If I could define exactly what that means, I'd out-Derrida Derrida. I'll try anyway and fail at it. Actually, that last sentence helps a lot: according to Derrida, language always fails in its quest for meaning. Derrida is a scary guy. Many traditional scholars are afraid that to embrace deconstruction would be the end of all meaning. "If meaning cannot be fixed"—they throw their hands into the air—"then all is chaos. If all the best minds are doing critical theory, who will create literature?"

This is how some of us are reacting to sport climbing: "If the best climbers spend all their energy on the sides of buildings, with fixed protection, in timed contests, who will climb the mountains?" It's not a very realistic fear, is it? Like any other unit of meaning, sport climbing is defined by its differences from other kinds of climbing. It shares much with other climbing, but it's the differences that matter.

Heraclitus famously declared that a man cannot step into the same river twice. Derrida might say that a word does not, *can not*, have the same meaning twice. Likewise, we know that it is nearly impossible to do the same climb twice. Too much changes—our partners, the weather, the physical nature of the route itself, our equipment. In sport climbing, the competitor very nearly steps into the same river as his or her fellow climbers.

I missed the big competition at Snowbird this year. Part of the reason was that I realized that my main motivation would have been to not miss something. The same motivation once kept me going to parties that I knew from experience would bore me, but if I didn't go maybe something great would happen and I would miss it. My wife at times has taken the opposite approach to sports—when asked if she wanted to go to a baseball game, she said, no, she had been to a baseball game once before.

The competition at Snowbird is an interesting show, a party, and I like parties and shows as much as the next person. A lot of people seem to confuse being part of a scene with climbing, and I just wanted to be sure I had it straight. The weekend came and went, and I got busy with deadlines and commitments—stuff I had to get done before I could get away to Jackson Hole. So I didn't make it up to Snowbird. I've heard that Raboutou blew them all away this year. I wouldn't have minded seeing it. If I want to, I'm sure I'll be able to read all about it, maybe even (God forbid) watch it on television.

The French have an expression, *à cheval*, which means, literally, on horseback. The French use it, and English-speaking climbers have adopted it, to describe traveling across a knife-edged ridge— straddling the crest with one foot on each slope. I've heard that in the Tetons, near the top of Irene's Arête, is a spectacular pitch that one crosses *à cheval*. I hope to be on it sometime next week. We can be astride issues, too, but one day we have to come off the ridge and stand on one side or the other.

1990

This essay was written when I was in the throes of graduate school and under the influence of literary theory. This is evident not only when I speak explicitly of the theorists but throughout. Today I am much less concerned with the language we use to label this or that. I am more of the "Vy cant't ve chust climb?" school of climbing led by John Salathé.

The great American climber Royal Robbins responded flatteringly to this piece with a letter to the editor of *The Climbing Art*, where the original appeared. Robbins, always highly principled, saw sport climbing as an abomination. This attitude was reflected in the then-popular bumper sticker that read "Sport Climbing Is Neither." A few years later, when I met Robbins, he remembered neither the essay nor his response to it. Such is literary fame!

Though I had been planning to climb Irene's Arête with Tom Huckin, we somehow never got to it. Later, we would climb the Snaz together, another of the great Teton classics; see the essay "Climber as Writer."

THE PURPOSES
OF ASCENT

Episodes and Conversations on Adventure,

Climbing, and What It All Might Mean;

An Account of Twenty Years in the West

Friday night in the dorms at Michigan State, February 1972. I am in my room, alone, reading. Not studying, reading; never one to let schooling interfere with my education. This scenario, no doubt tells bunches about my experience there. My roommate, the Arch, on the other hand, has hitchhiked back to Detroit to participate in the sexual revolution, or perhaps merely to celebrate his last days of freedom before his draft lottery number, 2, a near winner in any other game, sweeps him into the army and maybe across the Pacific to Vietnam. So I'm reading in my room; the door is closed. I'm not even open to whatever might happen here on a Friday night. Whoever they are and whatever they're selling, I'm not buying.

But there is a knock on the door.

Two large men fill the doorway. One of them is Big Keith, the Arch's father. The other man, larger even than Keith, has a worried expression on his face. They wear heavy overcoats and conspicuous, foreign-looking hats that look Russian. They look like no two men who ever walked into a college dormitory on a Friday night.

"Where is he?" Big Keith asks. And with this he stealthily removes his hand from his coat pocket. It's a private gesture, like a man on the street trying to hawk a watch, and in doing so he reveals to me the blue steel of a handgun. "I know he's your friend, David, but I'm here to kill the son of a bitch."

Big Keith had discovered the Arch's first-quarter grade-point average to be 0.0—a statistic that didn't jibe very well with his near-perfect SAT scores, and a feat he would soon duplicate in his second (and final) quarter. Big Keith and the Arch had a somewhat sloppy financial arrangement whereby Keith would supply the Arch with three signed checks at the beginning of the quarter—one each for tuition, room and board, and books. The Arch would buy hundreds of dollars' worth of books, then return them for a cash refund. He wouldn't be needing them. He asked me to tell him the last day to drop classes, and I did, but he was unable to summon the will to actually do it. He also asked me to wake him for dinner. After dinner he would trek to the liquor store for his daily case of beer. In the morning, when I woke, the Arch would often be sitting there drinking the last of his beers, the ever-present menthol cigarette between his fingers.

Big Keith and his sidekick stand there, taking up a surprisingly large chunk of floor space. I think I notice signs of relief in their faces, some great palpable weight lifted from their shoulders. Keith takes stock of the room, which is essentially bare, looking no doubt for some object on which to vent his anger. A single wall-hanging catches his eye—a Sierra Club poster titled *Ascent*—a photograph in which two climbers, Willi Unsoeld and Tom Hornbein, are approaching the west ridge of Everest on the '63 American climb.

"Who's *Ass-scent*?" he sneers.

I tell him it's mine. He nods, sits on the Arch's bed. He seems to have aged a decade or two in the few minutes he's been here. He's quiet a few moments longer, but the tension is undeniably gone from the room. "What am I supposed to do?" he asks. And I realized it wasn't merely a rhetorical question: he hoped I really might have an answer. But I didn't then and still don't.

This was the world I left when I moved west a couple years later. In Seattle, when people asked where I was from and I said Detroit, they might laugh, but they never wondered why I left.

That freshman year I read passionately, none of it assigned coursework. In the airless basement of the library in East Lansing, I found a shelf of *American Alpine Journals* and read them there on the floor. I found David Roberts's *Mountain of My Fear:* its foldout schematic of the west face of Mount Huntington inspires fear and longing to this day. In Jack Kerouac I read about a young man "on the dividing line between the east of my youth and the West of my future." And I took it personally. When I read Albert Camus's description of the existential landscape—"Everything horizontal, no relief; space is colorless, and life dead. Is it not universal obliteration, everlasting nothing made visible?"—I thought he might as well have been describing the view from my window, complete with Neil Young whining in the background, "Everybody knows this is nowhere." Finally, there was Dick Dorworth's classic *Night Driving.* Dorworth had held the downhill ski record for speed, and in *Night Driving* he crisscrossed the West in a blur of driving and skiing and climbing that exhilarated me and converted me to an unspoken, unacknowledged religion.

When I read *The Great Gatsby* for the first time, I was crossing the wheat fields of Saskatchewan on the way to the Canadian Rockies. Among the larger themes of the book are the despoiling of a continent and the contrast between the East and the West. I remember reading a description of the "middle-West" and not having a sense of where Fitzgerald was talking about. All I could think of was the midpoint between Baja and British Colombia. He was, of course, talking about Minnesota.

I just recently was introduced to Jon Waterman, the only person I've ever met who had a mental picture of the north ridge of Mount Kennedy and who therefore understood instantly what we had accomplished on the second ascent of the route in '77. Naturally, I liked him immensely. I had recently read and admired his essay on a winter ascent of Denali's Cassin Ridge in *The Best of Ascent*. The book contains the choices of longtime editors Allen Steck and Steve Roper, choices spanning twenty-five years of the magazine. Like self-proclaimed experts everywhere, Jon and I began to dissect their selections. We immediately and mutually lamented the omission of "Freaker's Ball" from the '74 issue.

Sometime later I realized my opinion of the story was based on a twenty-year-old memory; after all, in '74 I was a novice climber and semiliterate twenty-one-year-old. I dug out the old *Ascent*—to pass judgment not so much on the story but on the youth who had read it and kept its influence alive in his imagination over the years.

And the story did indeed turn out to have enduring power for me: success and death on Fitz Roy, one of Patagonia's most elusive summits. A party of young Americans manage to climb the legendary Supercouloir, but an accident on the descent takes the life of one. On the plane that carries him homeward after the tragedy in Patagonia, the young writer, Jeff Salz, tries to explain why to a rational physician from Indiana who harasses him. The physician defies him to explain himself and this climbing thing; Salz's answer is equally his attempt to explain the death of his best friend. Reading the words now, I recognize them as a young man's testimony, but none the less true for that. Perhaps my love of the piece has to do with the circumstances of my reading it for the first time, the fact that the writer described himself as a refugee "escaping imminent marshmallowism in the suburbs." Surely I must have seen myself in his description, though my own escape at the time was still in doubt.

I remember buying that *Ascent*. The receipt is still in its pages: Eastern Mountain Sports, North Conway, New Hampshire, six dollars. We had been trying to rent snowshoes for our planned traverse of the Presidential Range; it was the last week in December, and no snowshoes were available. We found this depressing until a guy sitting in a rocking chair—yes, an actual rocking-chair mountaineer—

told us it hardly mattered whether we had snowshoes, as our trip was destined to fail regardless. "Go on out and get it over with," he advised. "No one stays out for more than one night." This brightened our spirits considerably: if no one expected us to succeed, we had nothing to lose. We lingered in the store till closing, not having yet figured out where we would wait for a break in the weather. Walking out into the night air, we noticed first the cold, which was frankly terrifying, and then the clear sky—what we had been hoping for, but also secretly not hoping for. After all, you can't lose face if the weather is too bad to leave the trailhead. But now the moon was nearly full, the sky cloudless. We powered down a bagful of cheese-burgers and set out immediately, in the middle of the night.

Now, reading the contributors' notes in the same *Ascent,* I see that Todd Thompson says, "My purest climb still remains the north ridge of Mount Kennedy." And now, over twenty years later, I say to myself the exact same thing and realize that the psychic distance between myself and the boy-man who bought that '74 *Ascent* is great indeed. I reread Steve Roper's classic, "Dresden," in which he quotes the vow he made to himself fifteen years earlier (1959?): "I love climbing, it is the best of all possible activities, and I will climb, climb, climb for the rest of my natural life." This is the vow many of us made to ourselves, and it's hard now not to view my present life as a betrayal of it. Nonclimbers, I imagine, would view it differently: they would see the vow as the belief of a naive young man and fault us only for hanging on to the dream for so long. Fitzgerald describes Gatsby as springing forth from his Platonic conception of himself, adding that it was a conception formed as a seventeen-year-old.

In 1975 I moved from my hometown in Michigan to Seattle, Wash-ington, with the stated intention of making backpacks with Michael and Margaret Schonhofen. We rented a small, rundown storefront for sixty dollars a month at the north end of University Way and chained ourselves to sewing machines. There was no heat in the place, and the roof leaked. We loved it. Mike used to sing the Grateful Dead: "Make good money, five dollars a day, Make any more I might move away." We were happy just to be there. When the business died of natural causes, we split up the assets, such as they were, and though we went our separate ways businesswise, there was a much greater sense in which we've stayed close, like family, if you could choose your family.

Now, twenty years later, we were visiting the Schonhofens in Portland, where my wife, Aisha, was raised. There was an underlying sense of occasion (vague melancholy, too) about the visit, because later in the summer I would be moving back to the Midwest, closer to the home we had all left together. In 1975 we had felt that there was some infectious disease of the spirit endemic to the Midwest, and that were we to stay we would surely fall prey to it.

Mike said, "I got something I want to show you," and laughed as if under his breath: "Heh, heh, heh." We'd heard him say this before and knew that anything could happen. Mike might open a cabinet to reveal dozens of bottles of single-malt Scotch or some sort of custom-made hybrid bicycle constructed out of titanium and assembled by hand from parts collected around the world. Perhaps he was now building the airplane in his garage that he had been hinting at for years. But no, he was holding a videocassette. Mike had called me on the phone after seeing *Road Warrior*, describing it as the ultimate Detroit movie. Years later he would do the same with *Robocop*. Mike believes that the Apocalypse will begin in Detroit, and he'd prefer to be elsewhere when the action begins.

This video begins with earsplitting rock music and shows Mike walking across an empty parking lot dressed in some sort of nylon suit, which we shortly come to understand as a jumpsuit. We are going to watch a video of Mike jumping out of an airplane. It's an amazing, if crude, little video. Mike's story behind the video, of course was actually much more interesting: *Free Falling with the Hell's Angels*.

When the video is over there's a moment of silence which fills the space left by the obnoxious music. Aisha says, "I guess I don't get it. Can you explain the appeal of that to me?"

Like Aisha, I have never understood the appeal of jumping out of an airplane. But Mike is not the impetuous sort: I was sure he would know at least why it appealed to him. He pretended to be thinking so as to show some respect for the depth of the question, which had not in fact been made glibly. From his hesitation, I knew we would hear an answer much rehearsed in Mike's mind.

"It's a situation where actions have consequences, and you can't bullshit your way out of it. It's not like, 'Oh, well! I made a mistake.' That's the appeal—it's really simple. If you screw up, you die."

"And there's something comforting about that?"

"Yeah, there is. You're absolutely 100 percent accountable for your actions. It's one of the one true things."

Roy, too, was from the East. We lived in our Skid Road apartments at opposite ends of Seattle, working less-than-minimum-wage jobs and climbing every weekend. It was Roy who told me about Evergreen: he was enrolled for the fall, but he was keeping that a secret. Later we would become roommates down in Olympia. At the time Roy was working in a growing business and integral to its plans. But that life wasn't the one he had planned for himself. I remember his revelation—part conspiratorial, part confessional. We were on a rocky little summit in the Peshastin Pinnacles, the weather was mild, and we were unhurried. He made me promise not to tell anyone. He didn't want to be bribed to stay on in the business, I suppose.

"Evergreen is a place," he told me, "where you can design your own curriculum." And he told me about Willi Unsoeld, who was on the faculty there—the Unsoeld of my old poster, who with Tom Hornbein had made the most daring American ascent in the Himalaya, the West Ridge of Everest. I enrolled.

But once at Evergreen, I more or less avoided Unsoeld. I could see that he attracted the lost, many of whom were truly needy. My operating principle was that if I wanted to climb, I didn't need to be in school to do it. Then came this chance to go climbing in the St. Elias Range, and the only way I could swing it was to use school loan money. I came up with the idea of incorporating the climb in the Yukon into an academic project. I was somewhat alarmed at how easily I was able to convince faculty members of the integrity of my plan. I felt guilty and decided to talk to Unsoeld about it. That was like choosing to ask a priest if he thought the church was a good place to find spiritual guidance.

Unsoeld, the white-bearded patriarch, smiled at me. "First expedition, eh?" And he absolved me of any intellectual sins and sent me out the door with his blessing and a mini lecture on using fixed ropes. He also recommended that I read David Roberts's *Deborah: A Wilderness Narrative*, a harrowing account of two climbers on a dangerous unclimbed Alaskan route, made all the more miserable by a largely unspoken conflict that brewed between the men who began the climb as best friends.

My friend Sean O'Grady, in describing the difference between Thoreau's *The Maine Woods* and *Walden*, calls the former a "wilderness narrative" and the latter a "narrative wilderness." I came to realize that Unsoeld was cautioning me about the inward journey, the hard look into the narrative wilderness that is the self.

The summer I came back from Alaska, I was living in a real apartment in Seattle. It was beautiful, and I ate a lot of ice cream and savored the fact of having survived the climb in the St. Elias. I was in love, too, and I didn't very much feel like going climbing. Although it always sounded good to me, there always seemed to be some reason I couldn't go. I didn't have a phone in the apartment. I worked. And wrote.

One Sunday in the papers, I noticed a small article about missing climbers. It sounded so familiar: the Index Traverse, a climb Roy and I had driven by and dreamed aloud about dozens of times. At the end of the article the climbers' names were revealed, and they were Roy and D. Cliff. Trapped high up on Middle Index in a storm. A rescue was organized in Seattle, but no one had gotten hold of me, since I had no phone and all. The person who organized the rescue was a local character who was a likable enough egotist but is best remembered for a number of unseemly acts. The rescue effort was that person on his best day—the way I would like to remember him, the way we all would like to be remembered.

Roy described it all to me later. He and D. Cliff were trapped up high in bad weather. No way off. Waiting it out. No food. They kept their spirits up by taking turns offering to go out for food: "I'm going out for burgers and fries, can I get you anything?" and then laughing hysterically. They were pinned down under some wretched overhang somewhere among the summits of the arrowlike peaks in the North Cascades. There was nowhere to go.

Roy talked about finally getting off the thing. Two worn-out, hungry guys walking down some soggy fire road in the dark when a helicopter whirred in out of the black and someone asked them if they were all right. They hadn't known anyone was looking for them. It was adventure, see? They didn't know if they could do it or not, and on that particular trip they couldn't, but they were pushing it.

When I first met my wife, she claimed to notice a thing or two about my friends and me, transplanted Midwesterners and Easterners. We had a great concern for the equipment we used in the mountains. This was natural: we had all at one time or other been in the outdoor-equipment business. But my Aisha thought the whole outdoor-equipment business was unnatural.

"Just put on some clothes and go. Clothes that will keep you warm and dry and that you don't mind ruining. It's not such a big deal."

She thought our excursions were overplanned and silly. She was a "Just Do It" advocate long before it became a corporate catchphrase. The irony, of course, is that the corporation that recommends we just do it would prefer us to just do it after acquiring a pair of hundred-dollar specialty shoes.

Slide shows from our trips she found boring. She liked the images, but couldn't we just show them and move on, "not talk about them so much?" She once took a series of photographs of the near west side of Salt Lake City—streets she traveled every day. They became a slide show of about thirty images, and she set it to a Paul Winter song. It was a beautiful show, and it lasted about two minutes and twenty-one seconds.

Now, all these years later, I realize that at some point I stopped climbing with a camera. The reasons for this are clear. A camera is a nuisance while you're climbing. Most of the climbing shots we see today on the covers of magazines are taken by people who go to the mountains to shoot photographs. I admire these photographers for a lot of reasons, but mainly because they work hard at what they love, for very little money, with no assurance of actually taking a great photo or, if they do, of selling it. But there's a problem: we've become immune to greatness in these kinds of photos. This month's *Climbing* is a great example: Alex Huber on the Salathé Wall in Yosemite. A truly amazing shot—but wait a minute, who's taking the shot, and where from? Then you realize there's this other person there, this photographer, apparently suspended on some kind of contraption that gives him this particular point of view.

So yeah, I stopped taking my camera climbing: just one more thing to get in the way. Then, when I was on the verge of leaving the West, I started taking the camera again and kept the shutter clicking. This urge to document everything is a symptom of our absence from the thing itself, the unnaturalness of us in that exotic landscape.

When I think back to my days in Olympia, it feels like everyone I knew then was from the East or Midwest—newly arrived with the express purpose of reinventing themselves. Aisha and Woody Barmore are the obvious exceptions: true Westerners, though neither would emphasize anything of the sort. I am talking about a relationship to land and self that is ingrained, not learned or acquired. Some of the native Westerners I met were children of the suburbs and products of mass culture, as most of us were, so I suppose what I'm talking about is a certain state of mind I associate with the Westernness but not guaranteed by merely being native born.

THE PURPOSES OF ASCENT

Woody was raised in Moose, Wyoming, and had spent a little time in Logan, Utah, before coming to Olympia. He did not like freeways, and while he liked people quite a bit, he was uncomfortable around most of them. One night we were sitting around when one of Aisha's friends from Portland was visiting. She found us a little dull: we were all in a class together, and we talked about Wordsworth, Coleridge, and Melville. Aisha's friend wanted to talk about *the world!* She ended her spoken sentences with exclamation marks. "Wouldn't you love to go to the moon!" These were the days of the Apollo missions, and there was a national fervor in the air.

"Nope," said Woody. And he didn't elaborate. The friend was disappointed: we were dull. But what I knew was this—Woody's "nope" wasn't meant to be flippant or dismissive. It wasn't a refusal to entertain the notion of being in space or being on the moon. He had already thought about it and come to the same conclusion as Robert Frost in "Birches": "Earth's the right place for love / I don't know where it's likely to go better."

The first time I drove out to see Woody was to return something I'd borrowed. I had to leave campus, get on the freeway, and drive north almost to the delta where the Nisqually, burgeoning with meltwater from Mount Rainier's glaciers, flows into Puget Sound. Off the freeway I drove for six or seven miles. Nowhere along the two or three turns was there anything to indicate a human presence: no homes, buildings, roads into the brush—nothing. Finally I came to a row of mailboxes and some houses on a bluff above the shoreline. I walked down a trail through a tangle of thick northwestern greenery, past an outhouse, to a cabin—gray boards and red tarpaper roof. And Woody, happy king of his domain, said no one made the drive who didn't stay for dinner. He had fresh venison his brother had left with him and potatoes, green salad and tomatoes, homemade sourdough biscuits baked in the woodstove oven—"puppy bellies," Woody called them. We had beer and later whiskey. And I felt that somehow I had it all wrong up to that point.

Woody left the Northwest—too many people, he claimed—for

Wyoming while I was in the Yukon, and I lived in his cabin on Puget Sound for a year and a half while I finished school. Like Woody, I didn't put in a phone, only for me it was because I didn't want to pay for it, whereas I suspected for Woody it was simply another unnecessary machine. I tried to write there and was surprised to learn that solitude and beauty weren't at the essence of the writing process. It was many years later that I figured out that writing was a matter of language and time.

After I left the cabin for California, Scott Baker, a friend from the St. Elias trip, moved in and he put in a telephone, a new roof, improvements. And just weeks after I settled in Southern California, it was Baker who called me on the phone to tell me that Willi Unsoeld had died on Mount Rainier, swept away in an avalanche.

Baker lives on Puget Sound to this day. Woody's a hand logger now—all horses and ropes—back in Wyoming. We exchange Christmas cards, and we have pairs of kids the same ages. In the last letter we got, Woody said, "We're living in a house for the first time," and he marveled: "Man, houses are wide."

Every summer I climb with my friend of thirty years, John. This has been possible largely because I have lived in the West and climbed often, and he has had the money to fly to wherever I've happened to be living: Puget Sound, Southern California, Salt Lake City, Northern California. In the summer of 1981 we planned to climb the classic route on the east face of Mount Whitney, the highest peak in the lower forty-eight states. Because of some complication or other, I planned to take the bus up to Lone Pine, the southernmost of the highway mountain towns on the east side of the Sierra Nevada, and meet them at Whitney Portal, a literal gateway from the high desert of the Alabama Hills to the alpine forest that marks the beginning of the high country at around nine thousand feet. I remember now he was on a car trip with his girlfriend, soon to be his wife, M. They would be driving south from Yosemite. The rendezvous was smoothly accomplished, wilderness permits were secured; they had a cooler full of iced beer. Even the weather—cause of many climbing debacles in the past—looked fine.

At some point on their drive they had decided that M would accompany us as far as base camp at Iceberg Lake, a craggy moonscape beneath the east face at about twelve thousand feet. I had spent much of the previous summer climbing in the Alps above Chamonix, and John, who was living in Paris at the time with M, took the train down on occasion to climb on the weekends. I remember M not liking the feeling of being excluded from that climbing world John and I shared. And she was naturally curious, too.

This summer John and M were living in Washington, DC—at sea level. I had just spent the whole summer working on the east side of the Sierra at around 7,500 feet. The approach to the high camp was neither obvious nor short, and I honestly can't recall my reaction to the news that M would be joining us. I'm sure I was concerned about their ability to acclimatize to the altitude. Although M was high-spirited and sporting minded, there was a palpable fragility about her: I remembered a gruesome story about the crushing of one of her ankles and its reconstruction with steel pins. But since I enjoyed her company, I probably thought that we would be slowed but it wouldn't matter.

And, in fact, the approach hike went all right—a couple slightly tense moments of routefinding, lots of talus, a slow finish, altitude taking its toll, but all accomplished in reasonable time. Iceberg Lake is a remote spot but also a popular staging area: people milled about in a trance, dazed by altitude, eyes intent on the east face, which rose another 2,500 feet.

We were greeted by a Brit: "See those lads?" He pointed upward.

No, we did not see them. The hour was late, the face shadowy, and the temperature was dropping rapidly in the high, thin air.

"Those lads are in a bit of a pinch."

"Are they?" asked John.

"Indeed," he claimed, "Leader took a nasty fall. Cracked his noggin."

We could not yet see them, but could hear them, yelling down, apparently for help.

"They haven't moved for over two hours. We're getting worried."

"Yeah," I sighed. With the unexpected prospect of coordinating a rescue effort staring me in the face, I too began suddenly to feel weary. But there was no one to help. John and M were beat up, and the remaining Brits were, as they claimed, "knackered." It was determined that I would scramble up as far as I could and try at least to understand their shouts. I got very nearly to their height on easy ground but was still about a hundred feet away over terrain too difficult to negotiate without a rope.

"Can you get down on your own?" In the wind it felt like I was yelling underwater. Again, louder: "Can you get down on your own?"

"Yeah."

"By dark?"

"Yeah."

"How is he?"

"Okay. . . . Bleeding."

"What are you doing?"

"Resting."

These answers were good enough for me, even if I didn't believe they'd get down by dark, even if I didn't believe that a guy who had been bleeding for hours was okay.

Back at high camp John and M had been more or less overcome by altitude. They had managed to pitch the tent, and they lay inside with their eyes closed, as if unable to summon the energy to open them.

"How are they?" John asked, the words escaping like a moan.

"Screwed," I said, "How are you?"

"Also screwed," said John. To us this was funny, and we laughed. What was funny was the shared recognition that we had been in this situation before—wasted at the start of a climb. M, however, did not see the humor in our situation.

"I say," said John, "I do believe I've cracked my noggin."

He and I continued our idiotic laughing. "I guess you had to be there," I said to M.

"I am here," she said.

My offer to make dinner seemed only to exacerbate their moaning. John began crawling toward the tent entrance, mumbling, "I think I'm going to be . . ." He stuck his head out the tent and proceeded to vomit, pausing between surges to turn to us and grin. This too, John and I found hilarious. M exploded: "Now I see exactly why you two BIG FUCKING IDIOTS love this so much." Which caused us to laugh even harder and sent M into the fetal position inside the cocoon of her sleeping bag.

Later that night we heard the telltale sounds of clinking hardware: the accident victim had returned. Among the tangle of hardware and sleeping gear in their tent, there was much blood. It looked exactly like what it was: the scene of an accident. Someone ran down for help. There was nothing we could do. "Your job is to keep him awake," I said to his partner. "Apply pressure."

The next morning we awakened to the unmistakable *thwack thwack thwack* of helicopter blades. The thing hovered above, sending sleeping pads and down jackets into a dusty swirl. A door opened and a smoke bomb was hurled out to indicate wind direction for the landing. The helicopter landed and picked up the injured climber. His partners had done a curious thing: afraid of being charged for the cost of the helicopter rescue, they had abandoned their friend and hidden under rocks farther down the valley. They left the dazed man lying on a sleeping bag, his head wrapped in a bloody turban—a perverse offering of sorts.

Having observed this spectacle, we were not in much of a hurry to do the classic East Face route—the very route the Brits had fallen on—and after several cups of tea we decided instead to do the Mountaineer's Route, an easy scramble, the route of John Muir in 1873. The climbing presented little in the way of technical difficulties, and we felt a little small for our decision to, in effect, hike and not climb. It's an ego game: it's the difficulty of the route that matters, not the summit. We were, we liked to think, larger than peak baggers. No summit-at-all-costs for us. But once on the summit we asked ourselves: weren't we larger than those happy only when pushing their limits—wasn't it good just to be here?

Later, back at camp, M was not very impressed with much she had witnessed, except perhaps the stark beauty of the place—which was something, because in fact the beauty is so stark that not everyone can appreciate it. On the hike out to the road she twisted her ankle and had to be assisted down—just short of actually carried. This happened about eight miles from the car, turning a downhill stroll into something of an ordeal and stretching the afternoon toward darkness.

Later still, John and M's marriage lasted a mere six weeks. And much later than that, when John looked back, he refused to believe that his climbing was related to its brief duration.

But at this moment we found ourselves on the summit early in the day with a bar of chocolate and plenty of water, gazing out over Death Valley, its heat shimmering toward us in waves that never arrived, while Air Force jets buzzed the summit ridges in sheer exhilaration, and tiny Sierra finches, dazed by thin air and hunger, alighted on our fingertips and picked sunflower seeds out of our palms. "There are worse places to be," John noted.

I nodded in agreement: I could think of worse places.

"Hey, you're going to see something now," Steve Roper says. He's pointing to Allen Steck a few feet of ahead of us on the walk-off down Lovers Leap in the northern Sierra. We've just ascended the second of two rock climbs, moderately difficult classic routes, each three or four hundred feet long. Steck is down on all fours. He's going to drink water right out of the stream. "Can you believe this?" Roper asks, as if Steck is the last living man on the planet to perform such a foolhardy stunt.

Steck and Roper are the longtime editors of *Ascent*, home to the best mountaineering writing for about twenty-five years, starting in

1967. They also collaborated on *Fifty Classic Climbs in North America*, an almost instant classic, criticized by some, ignored by no one.

Fifteen years ago this would have been a commonplace occurrence throughout the American mountain West, but now the threat of giardiasis has ended the practice for all but a few diehards like Steck—who, I should add here, is sixty-nine years old. I should also add that Steck still leads 5.10, a level of rock climbing that at the time I learned to climb in the seventies was near the limit of the possible. He's also the best example I know of a person who appears to have personally dictated the terms of his own life.

So I can't drink out of streams anymore. I can't very easily dive into the ocean anymore either, since a student of mine broke his neck diving into a sandbar off Huntington Beach. How long will it take Steck to pick up the bug, anyway? He hasn't yet, and he's probably spent more time in the mountains than anyone I've known. On the other hand, my wife and children picked up giardia drinking tap water in Davis, California.

Which reminds me of the time *after* my expedition to the St. Elias. I had spent thirty-five straight days in the mountains, and the whole trip, viewed in retrospect from the comfort of my Seattle apartment, was a bit overwhelming. I did not feel compelled to climb. The summer went by. School started, and I was not climbing. Then a curious thing happened. I was in a car accident on an icy road. A car spun out of control in front of us and into our lane, where we hit it broadside at about fifty miles per hour. Did I say we were in a VW Bug? We were not seriously injured, but I hated the thought of such an accident ending my life. In a few months I was up on the Kautz Glacier on Mount Rainier: home, as John Muir claimed, in the mountains.

Back with Steck and Roper on the road to Lovers Leap: there is an accident on the road. Clearly it has happened just moments before, but enough people have stopped that we don't feel we could add anything.

Roper is affected by the sight. "That could be us," he says. "How could that have happened? Jesus, we're lucky." This reminds him about a recent climbing accident, which also scared him. The victim, a well-known climber, fell twenty-five feet and hit the ground, amassing various injuries, none life-threatening, but all painful sounding. "And on some shit climb too. Some inglorious little unimportant climb. It's not like it was the North Face of the Eiger—it's just not worth it."

"But for the Eiger North Face, it would be?"

"Maybe." And then he adds, "And he climbs every day too. Think what it means for duffers like us." (I'm thinking: probably a hundred years of climbing experience among us, with me only adding twenty.)

As we're roping up, the sound of helicopter blades fills the canyon. It's a sound we all associate with the airlifting of an accident victim. We're all feeling particularly mortal. Roper is thinking about merely observing, sitting in the shade all day watching the sun work its way across the wall. "I'm scared," Roper says. "Jesus. And I always have been. It's a miracle I did what I did." (What he did was climb over four hundred routes in Yosemite Valley.)

Moments later, when there's nothing left but to begin, it's Roper leading.

For a long time I didn't go to Yosemite Valley. During the years I lived in Southern California, we went to Tahquitz and Joshua Tree regularly, and most summers we did a Sierra climb or two. I climbed in the Cordillera Blanca and Chamonix in those years as well. So it might not have appeared that I was purposely avoiding Yosemite, but I was. I said it was crowded, and to a smaller circle of friends I said I knew I would never want to leave, so I'd just save myself the pain of leaving by never going there to begin with. But the real reason is that I wasn't ready for a grade VI climb, a big wall, and therefore I felt unworthy. Finally I got over it.

My last time there was just a week before I left for the Midwest, and it was an odd visit. I was with John again, and he was depressed.

He had good reason, but in the thirty years I had known him, this was the first time I had seen him that way. I didn't even quite realize this fact until this moment of typing it in. John is the most forward-looking person I know. We had been thinking of doing the classic Royal Arches route, but it was too long—meaning that even though it was easy, when you get high enough above the valley floor, you're committed to finishing the route—and anyway it was too hot for a south-facing route.

Instead, we made a half-hearted attempt at Nutcracker. There was a party just ahead of us, and they were slow. New Yorkers. I was thinking about the two New Yorkers, both named Mark, whom I had climbed Devils Tower with in 1975. I was on my way west, and these two kindly made their climb a threesome. We were slow. On the descent we got our rappel ropes caught on the rock, a common error on the Tower, and it was dark when we returned. We had been out of water for hours (a scenario I have since repeated on so many climbs that it's really kind of pathetic). Nonetheless, I remember thinking that now I was in the West and that even before I'd reached Seattle I had done a great climb. I took it as a sign of the great climbs to come. And it was.

These new New Yorkers on Nutcracker reminded me of myself twenty years earlier, except they were a lot more competent. They had bailed off the Arches the day before, after seven pitches. Nutcracker is about five rope lengths long, and I could see it would take them all day. The second climber was carrying enough gear to do an enormous wall—way too much. They had protected the first pitch extensively, every five feet, and each piece was a struggle to retrieve and required much shouting. After well over an hour, the second was only halfway up the first pitch. I climbed to the first possible belay spot. It was a hundred degrees in the Valley. This is a south-facing climb, too. With the heat and these guys in front of us, and a—how shall I say—*uninspired* partner, suddenly the climb lost its charm for us. We downclimbed the first pitch and headed back to the car.

We spent the day walking around the valley. Walking, not hiking. We talked. I carried a camera, not knowing when I'd be back. I took one photograph, of Glacier Point Apron. It's a shot I wouldn't have been able to take if I hadn't been merely walking around the valley. I didn't even feel guilty about not climbing. I guess I was just happy to be walking around the most beautiful place on earth with one of my oldest friends in the world, even if he wasn't so happy. We ended up at the Mountain Room Bar at a very early hour.

We drank steadily. The bar seemed to own only two tapes—U2 and Sting, a bad decade for music. Squirrels kept coming in the open doors and eating popcorn off the floor. The only other people at a table were two women, sixtyish, from Illinois, waiting for their husbands, who on a whim had decided to hike to the top of Yosemite Falls. I was thinking of the numerous times I had put my wife in that situation, and of the times I'd taken her with me instead, on excursions that were longer than they looked, or at least longer than I had promised, on which we had not enough water, on which we stumbled toward a car in darkness without a flashlight. I told these women that their husbands would be thirsty but that there was nothing to worry about until it was very dark—still hours off— and even then there wasn't too much to worry about.

There were very few people in the bar. Some tourists were waiting to be called over for dinner at the Four Seasons, a swank joint with linen tablecloths and silver place settings, unvisited by any climbers of my acquaintance. Steve Schneider, a famed Valley local and speed climber, walked in and stood at the bar. I had met him once: I climbed with his older brother Bob, an aging alpinist like myself, regularly at our local gym. Before I could talk to him, he began chatting up a young woman. I'm not one to interrupt such a scene.

In walked Peter Caster and girlfriend, Suzie: mirror images of one another, blond and bronzed. Peter had been traveling the sport-climbing circuit—Hueco Tanks, Rifle, Smith Rocks, Baja California—for a full year in a VW Beetle, and Suzie, a Canadian out of Vancouver, had been along for the last few months. I hadn't seen Peter in a long time; he had been my student at the University of California at Davis. I realized that once I moved to the Midwest the chances of random meetings like this would diminish greatly. Peter climbed hard routes, and we had always talked of doing one together, one I wouldn't be able to do with a partner of my own ability. We had talked of doing the East Buttress of El Capitan, first climbed the month I was born in 1953 by a four-man team—Bill Long, Will Siri, Allen Steck, and Willi Unsoeld. The route was a little wet still because the previous winter had seen the deepest snowfall in Sierra history, and the runoff continued late into July. It was clear it we wouldn't climb it this time. But seeing Peter in this charged atmosphere, I believed more strongly that one day we'd be there.

When we left the bar my spirits were high. I don't mean from drinking beer, although that probably contributed to it. I felt part of this great rarefied world. The night air was chilled and invigorating. The stars glittered above the shadows of Sentinel Rock and the other walls. I felt as if I was home.

The next morning we drove up to Tuolumne Meadows to attempt the classic southeast face of Cathedral Peak. The meadows were deserted because the campground was closed—again due to the record snowfall, which was slow to melt. But the little parking lot for Cathedral Peak was jammed. There, sitting in lawn chairs and drinking coffee out of insulated mugs, were David Reid and friends. They had been sitting there watching parties strike out for the classic, and for themselves they had decided on a less populated venue, one that did not require an early start, waiting in line, or worrying about rockfall from careless climbers above. David had taken it upon himself to function as the valet of the lot. He would leap—all six foot four of him—out of his low-slung, aluminum-framed chair greeting climbers, informing them of the number of climbers ahead of them, pointing out the trail if they didn't know it, and wishing them well.

And there were a lot of people up there. But the belay ledges were large, the weather perfect. Where would one rather be?

My twenty years in the West follow the roaring lifeline of freeways from Seattle south on I-5 to Olympia, continuing south to Southern California, north on I-15 to Salt Lake City, and west on I-80 to Davis, California. The schematic forms a sort of inverted triangle, almost an upside-down number 4. Of all the transitions, it was perhaps most difficult to leave Salt Lake, where the mountains are a daily presence.

Davis, in the Central Valley of California, is flat; you could stand on a beer can and see from one end to the other. Lovers Leap was less than two hours away, Yosemite four. There was a good low-key gym in town and climbers about. In the three years we were there, our second son was born. My position at the university was tenuous, and I had to work hard to find some security. We were broke. These were not the years in which a lot of climbing got done. I remember riding my bike home from work: the overpass that rose over I-80 was the high point of the trip, possibly the topographical high point of the city. From there one could look east to the Desolation Wilderness area, and on a clear day Pyramid Peak distinguished itself among the peaks that form the eastern horizon.

One day Sean O'Grady and I had traversed that ridgeline, descending back to the car as the crow flies to avoid making an eighteen-mile day even longer. I remember walking across a snowfield telling Sean about this winter climb we had tried up in the North Cascades. How we had tramped up this north face in snowshoes, Rainier Burgdorfer yelling at the top of his lungs: "I was made for this!" The conditions were a whiteout most of the day, and we never even really got a sense of where we were, much less how close we got to the top. When Rainier was sounding his barbaric yawp, D. Cliff and I didn't know quite what to think: Made for *what*, exactly? After I'd told O'Grady about this, he would exclaim the opposite at appropriate times, like faculty meetings or the beginning of semesters: "I was not made for this!" As if through the process of elimination, what we were made for would manifest itself.

Now, on my bike, cresting the overpass, the Desolation Wilderness was there, but I couldn't imagine the next time I would be free to be in it. Desolation was as close to me then "as the moon to a star," as F. Scott Fitzgerald said of the unreachable.

Now that I'm back in the Midwest, the mountains have become for me once again the boundaries of imagination. I think of the journey as a circle that does not close—it's five hundred miles further east to my parents' home. But there's nothing circular about the road—it's a straight out-and-almost-back. I wish to fix the coming and going precisely in my mind.

In returning I do not feel myself to be, as Fitzgerald described it, a boat "against the current, borne back ceaselessly into the past." I think more of Thoreau and his dictum that "if one advances confidently in the direction of his dreams, and endeavors to live the life which he has imagined, he will meet with a success unexpected in the common hours." A life of quiet desperation need not necessarily be a function of place. The mountains aren't going anywhere, and I'll have many fine days in them.

An even more often-cited line from Thoreau is: "In Wildness is the preservation of the world." It's also often misquoted—"wilderness" being substituted for Thoreau's "Wildness." And I have even misquoted it here myself. The sentence begins not with "In," but with "The West of which I speak is but another name for the Wild." So Thoreau wished to conflate the West with the Wild, whereas in memory I wish here to collapse *Westmountainsclimbing*.

Through a quirk of logistics I found myself driving I-80 twice this summer—both times west to east. The first time, driving across Wyoming with my family, my four-year-old kept asking, "Are we still in the cowboy West?" And we said yes, right up until we dropped into Nebraska, a descent that feels more abrupt than topography alone can account for. The second time I was alone, brooding and, through a packing mix-up, listening exclusively to the Grateful Dead. I can't say I didn't worry about returning to the Midwest, but I wasn't going to the Midwest I knew, I was going to the next place—forward, to the future. In Montana I noticed a curious topographic feature—going westward, one crosses the Continental Divide and then crosses it again! How is it possible? Where are we when we're between the Divides? Where we always are, but more so, I suppose.

I cross the Mississippi and am an hour and a half from my family and new home. I haven't seen my children in a month, and they're at an age when they're learning language at exponential speed—a month is a long time. The last seventy miles or so are on a country road, through cornfields and small farm towns: Preemption, Viola, Monmouth. Over the radio I hear a the flat voice of a disc jockey talking about the death of a star, and before any names are mentioned I realize it's Jerry Garcia, which saddens me greatly and, I think, confirms my post facto rationalization that California is no longer California. I'm thinking of Raymond Carver, a Western writer if ever there was one, and a writer whose topography is nonetheless always interior. His last published fragment asks:

> And did you get what
> you wanted from this life, even so?
> I did.
> And what did you want?
> To call myself beloved, to feel myself
> beloved on the earth.

I drive on, through the humidity of my youth, the heat shimmering off the pavement in waves, anxious to be with my family, home, on earth.

1997

This essay was written in 1997 as I was moving from the West, where I felt very much at home and had lived for twenty years, to a university position in rural west-central Illinois. I was feeling nostalgic and melancholic for the world I was leaving behind and uncertain about the future.

We stayed in the rural Midwest for thirteen years, many of them happy. In the early years there, I found summer work with the U.S. Forest Service in the eastern Sierra. My children learned to love the mountains, and between our trips west, gym climbing, rock climbing at the Mississippi Palisades, and my kids' enthusiasm for snowboarding, we managed to keep the dream of a mountain life alive.

Peter Caster and Suzie, whose last name I never knew, would marry briefly and, after her green card was secured, implode disastrously.

What I couldn't know when I wrote this essay was how close I would remain to the people I wrote about then: that John McInerney and I would continue to climb together almost yearly. He reminds me that the real punch line of the story about M at Mount Whitney was that after years of not speaking about it, we were huddled miserably under some rock in the rain high on some peak, climbing plans dashed, and that I invoked M's words: "Now I see why . . ." and then we laughed like lunatics. Nor could I foresee that Woody Barmore and I would take our kids on an extended climbing road trip and that the kids, too, would remain friends; that David Reid, parking lot greeter extraordinaire of Cathedral Peak, would visit Alaska just last month and we would climb Wolverine Peak together on a spectacular winter day.

CLIMBER
AS WRITER

From the Armchair

to the Tetons

On my first climbing trip to the West, we had maybe one day of good weather when it would have been possible to climb. We were poised at the Lower Saddle between the Grand and Middle Teton. Our plan was to first ascend Middle by the north ridge and then do the Grand. We had a copy of Leigh Ortenburger's guide, which we felt privileged even to own—it was a yellow-covered temporary edition. Reading it was another thing. No, that wasn't the problem. We could read it all right, we just couldn't match the words on the page to the terrain we could see. We wandered up to where we thought the route should be, but we never for a moment felt like we were on anything like a route. Finally, we scrambled back down, conserving our energy for the next day's attempt on the Grand. The arrival of winter that night kept us from repeating the scene on a trickier route on a larger peak. In four weeks we hadn't reached the top of a single mountain. My friend John McInerney had a hundred-dollar car that was missing teeth in its flywheel, so we drove back to Michigan without turning off the ignition. It was a great trip.

I never thought that reading about climbing was anything like the act of climbing, but it is a mistake that people apparently make. Otherwise why would litigation-conscious magazines and catalogs be compelled to print disclaimers?

My favorite is the first sentence from *Rock & Ice*'s disclaimer, appended to their guide section: "It is impossible to perfectly describe the real changing world and what each person's experience will be in it." It's true of course, but ironic: a magazine's goal is to work against this impossibility. This one from a recent Black Diamond catalog is more typical: "Books and catalogs like this one can help, but they are no substitute for personal instruction by a qualified person well versed in all appropriate safety techniques."

But climbing literature is hardly limited to guidebooks and catalog copy. More people are climbing than ever before, though not all of them would necessarily agree on what climbing is. The more participants, the more who attempt to write about it, the larger the reading audience. But what of the writing? Is more better? Is all this writing about the mountains good writing? People agree less on this than on what climbing is.

I remember when Jeremy Bernstein's portrait of Yvon Chouinard, Yosemite pioneer and founder of the Patagonia outdoor gear company, appeared in the *New Yorker*. It was the highly polished writing typified by the *New Yorker*: clear prose and impeccable style. Yet I had a friend, a climber and also a reader of the *New Yorker*, who claimed that the article was bogus. His judgment was based on a bungled description of how jumars operate. Jumars are ratcheted devices that clamp onto ropes and slide in one direction only; they have a number of uses for climbing and would be tricky to describe to any audience not already familiar with them. For my friend, this inaccurate description invalidated the whole article: the writer, he claimed, simply didn't know what he was talking about. It was clear to me that the writer knew very well what he was talking about, but that an editor other than the author had messed up the description of jumaring (yes, it's a verb, too!) in an attempt to render it in "clear prose." Climbers can be a tough audience. We're all experts, or so we think, suspicious of "outsiders" speaking for us.

I've encountered this same attitude occasionally with regard to a novel called *Solo Faces* by James Salter. I think it is the best novel about climbing yet written by an American. However, among climbers there is a strange resistance to it. Why? Because, they think, who is James Salter? What routes has he done? Who has he climbed with? Did you say he's a writer, has written screenplays? Well, no wonder.

Ironically, Salter himself is tough on the book. It is loosely based on the life of Gary Hemming, a larger-than-life climber who made his reputation on a famous rescue in the Alps and later took his own life. Salter himself has always felt that the book doesn't measure up to the real-life Hemming. In other words, Salter reads his own book like a climber might! The reader who has never heard of Hemming may perhaps admire the book more. Perhaps the more one knows about the real history, the less one admires the fictional re-creation.

One scene I felt was a stretch had Rand, the Hemming-based character, playing Russian roulette with his old climbing partner, now confined to a wheelchair. I remember thinking please, spare me the Hollywood melodrama. Only recently, upon reading Pete Sinclair's *We Aspired* (which I'll discuss later) did I learn that Hemming apparently really did play Russian roulette with Barry Corbet, crippled in a helicopter crash. Double irony: the moment that rang false to me did so not because it was a fictional creation (because it isn't exactly that). Rather, the scene's shortcomings seemed aesthetically out of place: they didn't fit the art. Fiction tells us what might have been, and Salter sweetly grants Hemming the reprieve Hemming never granted himself: a life after climbing. Rand survives his demons and lives on in flat desert obscurity.

In his recent address to the Montagna Avventura 2000 Conference, David Harris, a novelist and former editor of the *Canadian Alpine Journal*, makes some interesting observations about the evolution of mountain writing. He defines climbing writing as a true "ghetto literature," written only by climbers and essentially inaccessible to anyone but climbers. Aside from the mistaken usage of *ghetto*—after all, climbers choose their lives, not so ghetto dwellers—there is some truth to Harris's observation. But it is a truth that goes against the grain of a writer's instinct. Ludwig Wittgenstein, in his introduction to the *Tractatus Logico-Philosophicus,* said, "Perhaps this book will be understood only by someone who has himself already had the thoughts that are expressed in it—or at least similar thoughts." But having said that, he devoted his life to writing as clearly as possible. As writers, we try to avoid the old excuse for the failed punch line, "I guess you had to be there." In fact, our words are supposed to stand in for being there: we know it's a poor substitute, doomed to failure, but the attempt is to create—for those who have only the authority of our words—our world for them.

Lifting my pack at the Lupine Meadows parking lot, I reminded myself that this feeling isn't déjà vu. I really have done this before. A mile or so into the hike, we met Mike Friedman just finishing a traverse that began with Teewinot, traversed over Mount Owen, and ended with the North Face of the Grand Teton. Mike is an acquaintance from college who works summers as an Exum guide, a prestigious gig in our little universe; Exum is the oldest, most experienced guide service in the United States.. For a few summers, I'd bump into him every year either at Jenny Lake or at Dornan's, where the view of the Tetons from the bar window is unsurpassed, and we'd talk about our mutual friends, one of whom is Jack Lewis. It was, in fact, Jack who was just behind him on the trail.

It has been many years, ten or more, since I have seen Jack, but ours is the kind of friendship that time does not seem to interfere with much. In the seventies we had been on a thirty-five day climbing trip together, in and out of the St. Elias Range on skis. There were five of us, and we didn't see anyone else the whole time. We accomplished a superb climb, and the beauty and power of the experience were such that I never expect to repeat. So when Jack appeared around the corner of a switchback that morning in the Tetons, it was a kind of ecstatic reunion. It was so fine to see him, I don't remember what we talked about, if anything. We just sort of looked at each other with goofy grins on our faces, coexisting once again in that St. Elias world that the sight of one another conjured from memory.

But writers' relationships with their readers are at the far end of the spectrum from those of the climbers who have shared intense days in the mountains. Writers strive to share a memory with a reader who has not experienced the same events as they have. They must therefore cast a wider net, one that includes the climber-reader, for whom the written word works as a public record, but extends further to the armchair climber, for whom the whole, glorious vertical world must be evoked.

Climbers are a peculiar audience: sometimes easy to please, other times impossible. One of the great measures of writing's appeal to its audience, according to Aristotle, is the writer's ethos: not ethics, but personal authority for speaking about the subject. Thus, for the climber-reader, a climber who is well known is ipso facto a good writer. This can lead to statements in book reviews like "Three hundred pages of Ament and Robbins is one of the few things that could possibly upstage the Salathé Wall," or "Ament, however is beyond critique. How can one be critical of one so supremely self-confident?" What can we learn about the book or even the reviewer's opinion of the book from such statements? Unless we have an a priori respect for the ethos of the reviewer, all we can glean from a review of this sort is the reviewer's enthusiasm, which appears somehow misplaced.

But ethos is a legitimate reason to be moved by a piece of writing. I doubt that many people would take up the case for Jim Bridwell's being a great literary stylist. But he doesn't need to be; his written work rests on the authority of his considerable experience. So when you read "Dance of the Woo-Li Masters," the story of his ascent with Mugs Stump of the Moose's Tooth, the question of how well it's written is not particularly relevant: it's written as well as it needs to be. Joe Simpson's *Touching the Void* is another, better-known example. The elements of the tale are so harrowing it would be hard to mess up the telling of it: the cut rope, the abandonment, the miraculous survival, the hallucinatory crawl back to base camp. Experiences so powerful are being conveyed that the writing draws no attention to itself; it exists as a transparent window to direct experience.

Camp 4: Recollections of a Yosemite Rockclimber, Steve Roper's superb new history/memoir, provides a nearly perfect example of matching the ethos of the writer to the writing task at hand. The undertaking was a huge one, to be sure: the chronicling of Yosemite rock climbing from 1933 through 1970. In the first sentence of his preface, Roper claims, "I avoided writing this book for many years, thirty to be exact." What he doesn't tell us, our reading experience soon bears out: that those thirty years were also spent, in effect, *preparing* to write this book.

Roper began to lay the groundwork with "scores of route descriptions on scraps of paper and napkins" and the "ultra-detailed notebooks" recorded in preparation for his first climbing guide, published in 1964. Climbers' guides are certainly a kind of bare-bones history, answering for the reader most of the journalist's questions: who, what, when, where, and how? So it's a natural evolution, I think, for the exacting guidebook writer to craft a more ambitious history like *Camp 4*; after all, he has the best sense of what's been left out of the extant record.

Furthermore, current guidebooks seem to have abandoned most of the journalist's questions and settled in favor of the purely practical matter of answering only the "what and where." This trend makes a book like *Camp 4* all the more necessary. Roper is never content to merely list climbs by the facts of their first ascent: dates, names, and locales. After all, this was the flaw of the history books of our youth: history was presented as something "learned" by rote memorization, the very reason many of us came to despise it. Instead, Roper proceeds as a good historian must, by putting events and people into context and making careful (and convincing) judgments of their significance. While it may be possible for some of those characterized to differ with Roper's conclusions, his scholarship is remarkable, and his meticulously documented sources (thirty-seven in one chapter!) range from published journals to personal letters, unpublished manuscripts, and conversations, the latter three all recorded by date.

Someone else may have been able to put significant climbs into historical perspective, but I doubt that many observers would notice, as Roper has, that Chouinard and T. M. Herbert's first ascent of the Muir Wall was the first route on El Capitan to be done without fixed ropes by a team of two, the first to cross an existing route, the first to be done without a lengthy reconnaissance beforehand. And this is a randomly chosen example, one of many to benefit from the perspective of both the passage of time and the writer's astute analysis. As Roper notes, "What if we had written a book when only four routes existed on El Capitan?"

When I mentioned the journalist's questions I deliberately left out Why?, not just because I was speaking of guidebooks, and Why? has never been the guidebook's domain, but also because when asked with regard to climbing, it is so rarely answered to anyone's satisfaction. We often find others' answers lacking but are hardpressed ourselves to improve on them. Roper overcomes this problem by allowing many of the major players to speak in their own voices: many climbers, many reasons for climbing. So if the reasons for Yosemite climbing in the early sixties are diverse and somewhat nebulous, this account of them nonetheless rings true in some larger sense.

Roper's admission that "present beliefs about the past can significantly alter our perceptions of long-ago events" seems to have been taken up as a kind of operating principle, and the resulting sense of balance is evident throughout. When he has biases, he announces them to the reader, and the effect is that we are all the more convinced we're reading the truth, even though he's warned us that his choices are subjective.

Perhaps the book's finest achievement is the fine balance struck between its missions as both a comprehensive history and a personal memoir. Roper acknowledges that "by purest happenstance, unless one believes in divine intervention, I lived in Yosemite Valley's Camp 4 during the 1960s." Although he had done over 260 climbs in the Valley by 1963, Roper rates few of these as worthy of mention. Yosemite climbing would have evolved without Roper, but its collective memory so accurately and beautifully evoked here would not have. If Roper was lucky to have lived in the Valley in the sixties, we, his readers who did not live in the Valley, are luckier still.

Many years after our first attempts, McInerney and I finally climbed the Exum Route. In the years between our first attempt and the last, there had been another failed attempt, a drenching night and socked-in morning at the Lower Saddle. During the attempt on which we finally reached the summit, we watched ourselves climb as if it were happening to someone else. The named features of the route, familiar from years of reading, appeared as abstract concepts materializing before us: the Eye of the Needle, Wall Street, the Friction Pitch—each one charged with history.

Pete Sinclair, like Roper, lived in a golden age of American climbing, and like Roper's book, his memoir of the climbing life in the Tetons, *We Aspired: The Last Innocent Americans*, ends around 1970. Though both books balance personal memoir with a larger history, their approaches couldn't be more different, with Sinclair far more introspective and personal, gesturing, sometimes wildly, toward deeper meanings. Taken together, the two works comprise an incredibly comprehensive portrait of climbing during the sixties in the American West.

As a twenty-three-year-old climber in 1959, Pete Sinclair was quoted in *Time* magazine as saying: "You can't describe climbing to people. They don't have anything to compare it with." Nonetheless, his recently published book describes climbing about as well as can be done. If I say it is well written (and I do), what do I mean? And how do I prove it? I remember a moment when I was a high school teacher explaining to a parent his teenaged son's writing problems. The parent looked at me. "You mean *handwriting*?" he asked.

Sinclair's memoir begins with his ascent of the South Face of Denali in 1959, then recounts summers of mountain rescue work in the Tetons during the sixties. But it would be an oversimplification to say that this is what the book is about. Sinclair is writing about his life during this time. As such, the book probably has more in common with a coming of age story like *Portrait of an Artist as a Young Man* than with Maurice Herzog's *Annapurna* (which incidentally Sinclair cites as a "text of moral instruction"). But every autobiographical narrative about climbing can be said to be about the writer during a period of time. What's so special about Sinclair's version?

In most climbing books, the climbing is central; what it might mean, if anything, is often tacked on, hastily, it would seem. In other words, larger meanings seem to come as after-the-fact rationalizations by the writer. Sinclair doesn't tell us what events mean, as in the formulaic "Climbing leads to personal growth." Instead, he shows us how for him this leap has been accomplished. One chapter opens: "We have precious times when we glimpse the trajectory of our lives, when we are free enough from the nudge of things done and the tug of things to do to have a gravity-free movement of lucidity about what we are up to." This must also describe the space from which Sinclair's whole book arises, and also, I think, suggests the shortcomings of other works about climbing, which often feel as if their raison d'être is to "professionalize" climbing for the writer, to enable the climber to earn a living from climbing by writing about it, thus enabling future climbs.

Sinclair's book comes twenty years after the last events it describes have taken place. Events, people, landscape, movement, and emotion percolated in memory for years until Sinclair could find their essences in language. In this way, *We Aspired* reminds one of Norman Maclean's *A River Runs through It*: a book that was worth waiting for, until the author could set it down just right.

In the end, Sinclair leaves the Tetons, and, as you might guess from the subtitle, *The Last Innocent Americans*, there's a sense of melancholy to the departure, brought on by the deaths of friends (and strangers), as well as the increasing bureaucratization of the National Park Service. Still, when you stake a claim to being the "last innocent," you're marginalizing the experience of those who follow you. In fact, they may not be following at all, only finding their own way, as young, adventurous souls must always do.

It's obvious that climbing and writing are two radically different endeavors. It should be equally obvious, then, that what one might seem to have learned by reading is of limited value when actually climbing. Historical precedents for this view abound. In *The Sun Also Rises*, Ernest Hemingway's narrator ridicules another character for being influenced by W. H. Hudson's *The Purple Land*, "a sinister book if read too late in life."

In *Memoirs of a Mountain Guide*, Lou Whitaker observes that after Roper and Allen Steck's *Fifty Classic Climbs in North America* came out in 1979, there was a noted increase in climber deaths on Liberty Ridge, a classic route on the north side of Rainier. He goes on to say that rescuers almost always found a copy of the book in the climber's pack. The implication is the same as Hemingway's: it's a variation on the worn maxim "A little learning is a dangerous thing"—"a little *book-learning* is a dangerous thing." Both writers are seemingly forgetful that they're airing this view in written language, in a book, the impact of which will be precisely the opposite of what they claim to value: the readers will be influenced by . . . a book. Whitaker, at least, tries to put it into a larger perspective: "The deaths were not caused by that book or any other, but by inexperienced climbers seeking the glory of doing a classic climb."

Whitaker is a first-rate raconteur, and one of the great charms of his book, for the reader who has met him, is that his voice can be heard in the written prose. Sometime after his book appeared, Whitaker told the story of a midnight rescue call from Mount Rainier and being helicoptered up to one of the high glaciers, where a broken-legged climber has wrapped himself in his down sleeping bag awaiting salvation. Whitaker describes approaching the bag, uncertain whether the man is dead or alive. A face appears out of the bag, and the injured climber's first words are: "I've read your book." In telling the story Whitaker laughs his great laugh, as he must have at the scene: "Well," he says, "you sure didn't read it too good!"

The last time I climbed in the Tetons was a couple seasons ago, when I did the Snaz with Tom Huckin. It was the culmination of a few seasons of climbing together, a partnership that we knew would soon change when I left Salt Lake City. Doing the Snaz was Tom's idea. A classic rock route first put up in the sixties, it still has a reputation, even though its grade is now thought modest. For us, it was not so modest but right at the edge of our abilities.

I had been in the Wind River Range and was a bit tired physically and tired, too, of the weather, which couldn't seem to make up its mind as to which season it attended, summer or winter. The previous day, John McInerney and I had made the long hike up to Symmetry Spire, only to be chased off by lightning and a hard rain that struck so quickly we were soaked to the skin before we could even don raingear. That night I was to rendezvous with Huckin, who was newly arrived in Jackson Hole and undeterred by my description of the weather. We found ourselves sorting gear a couple hours before daylight in the parking lot at the Death Canyon trailhead.

As we approached the climb, a herd of elk thundered by us in the dark, and twice we had to skirt moose that held their ground on the trail. Although it was late season, the river roared down the canyon; I noticed a living fir tree about a hundred feet long lying haphazardly in the torrent, having been uprooted by some primeval force. Soon we were on the route, the long open book first written on by Yvon Chouinard and Mort Hempel. The morning's promise of good weather held all day. Though we made steady time, long blocks of hours disappeared into the effort. As on many of the best climbs, we didn't manage to take many photographs. There are a couple from the crux pitch, Tom's lead. The first shows him standing on a large, detached pillar fifteen or so feet away, the sky a wedge of blue above the dihedral. The second shows him a hundred feet up, unrecognizable, the clouds in the sky completely refigured in the time it had taken him to move up. By the time we found ourselves on top, the sun had gone beyond the hanging valley to the west. By the time we made it down to the packs, it was dark. The trail was still negotiable, but we were tired, and it was late. Once again the herd of elk thundered by, and soon the lights of the valley began to appear. We drove back to Tom's sister's ranch, where we ate steak and drank a couple of beers out of longneck bottles, giddy as kids in cowboy hats. It had been perfect, the kind of day you read about.

1992

The arc I tried to imagine here is from a mere reader to someone who can not only read the mountains but also read the words used to describe them and understand what they mean. The four climbing moments recalled from the Tetons were intended to hold together the reading of three or four books by or about climbers. These books came out at roughly the same time (except for *Solo Faces*, the only fictional work, which came out much earlier). I meant my thoughts about them more as a homage to the writers as my teachers (and Pete Sinclair was indeed my teacher at Evergreen State College).

In Jeff Long's recent collected fictions, *Too Close to God* (Imaginary Mountain Surveyors, 2015), he claims, "Ascent is a physical act, of course, but not before it is an idea built from other ideas, like mountain and summit. We climb upon our language." Or, as was said a few millennia ago: "In the beginning was the Word."

LAST DANCE OF
THE WU LI MASTER

A Distanced Appreciation

of Terrance "Mugs" Stump

There are these mystics wandering about all our mountains. Not too many of them. It is very likely that a few of
them get themselves killed in any given year. They don't
make big headlines when they do, because nobody but a
few other hard men know who they are or how they die.

—John Jerome, "The Hard Men," *On Mountains*

I didn't personally know Mugs Stump, who died last year [1992] on
Denali at the age of forty-one, except in the way the New Testament
claims: "By their deeds you shall know them." I have a deep respect
for his deeds. In the early eighties I taught school with L, the quintessential armchair mountaineer. He worshipped Chris Bonington as
someone might who relies on book knowledge for an understanding of the game. I remember when *Outside* published an article on
the ascent of the North Buttress of Mount Hunter by Mugs and Jim
Bridwell, calling it the Last Great Problem—or, to give the writers
their due, perhaps they called it the Last Great *Alaskan* Problem.
Either way, it was one of the last times I remember a climb being

described in those terms. L came in raving, flecks of spit flying in excitement: "You gotta love this guy Mugs Stump. Can you believe this guy?" L had found himself an American hero.

I can't help crazily juxtaposing Mugs and Jay Gatsby, the great American fictional hero who died young. Nick Carraway, the narrator of his story, speculates that Gatsby "paid a high price for living too long with a single dream." But who's to say what is too high a price?

> Nonclimbers start calling climbers masochistic mystics with overwhelming death wishes; climbers maintain that nonclimbers simply don't understand. It is not that the truth lies somewhere in between these irreconcilable viewpoints; it is that the truth is unavailable.
>
> —John Jerome

After I moved to Salt Lake City, I'd see Mugs around from time to time, though I still didn't know him personally. The first time I saw him, he was hanging out in the local shop, a great mountain gear shop, in which it's often not possible to distinguish the employees from the people hanging around reading magazines and eating Mexican from the nearby fast-food place. He was talking about routes in the Cathedral Spires in Alaska. He was making them sound like afternoon bouldering problems, no doubt to appeal to his audience of predominantly sport climbers. Mugs was relaxed, no hard sell here, and at the same time I thought his expression "focused"—faraway perhaps, but with nothing dreamy about it. I didn't sense that the younger climbers who were listening had any desire to do an Alaskan grade VI, precisely because they knew what was involved: deprivation, exhaustion, frostbite, and objective dangers. I can't blame them—after all, I probably have more in common with them than I did with Mugs. And while I admire them, the sport climbers who work for a month on a sequence of 5.12d moves, my admiration is more like what I have for a professional tennis player.

It sounded to me as if those young climbers were humoring him. Sure, they had a genuine interest; they enjoyed hearing his descriptions, but they were only window shopping, at best. Around the same time, I remember hearing a young guy at the same shop ask: "When are you going to get rid of these bogus mountaineering photos and put up some pictures of real climbing?"

The second time I saw Mugs was just last fall, one of those greater examples of synchronicity that makes you think, against overwhelming evidence, that there really is some sort of plan at work (whose plan it is, and what it might mean, remain in essence unknowable). I was at the bakery. That very day I had read in a newly arrived magazine that Mugs had soloed the Cassin Ridge on Denali in fifteen hours. The mere thought of it blew me away: the commitment, the speed. I have thought about the Cassin, studied Bradford Washburn's photos, had a sense of what is involved. I felt inspired by Mugs's achievement: not inspired to make immediate plans to do the Cassin (much less solo it), but just to know there was someone out there who had done it. I felt privileged just to understand the magnitude of his accomplishment. The account added that Mugs's current home was his van in Salt Lake.

Hours later, I walked to the bakery pushing my infant son in the stroller. There was Mugs waiting in line, longish hair streaked with gray. I thought twice before complimenting him on the Cassin: it was October, months after the fact. I was a geek with a kid in a bakery, getting ready to load up on far more carbohydrates than I would be burning off anytime soon. Plus, I never knew how to actually pronounce Cassin—would my tendency to pronounce all foreign words as if they were Spanish betray me here? Finally, I did speak, telling him I admired the route and that soloing it was a truly amazing achievement, all the time thinking, "Is this what L feels like?" I held back from saying I thought I might like to do the Cassin someday, thinking about how whenever someone introduces you as a writer, one in two people respond by saying, "I always wanted to write a book," and if you're lucky they leave it at that. I told him I climbed on weekends and used to climb a little more. Mugs was modest—there was nothing really for him to say. I watched him drive off in his van and gave my son a raisin breadstick to occupy him on the walk home, half a mile, my only exercise of the day.

The last time I saw Mugs was at the Black Diamond open house. Black Diamond is a climbing-hardware company that had recently been divorced from its parent company, Patagonia, and had moved from California to Salt Lake City. Many well-known climbers were there. I knew only the local people and a few others by sight and reputation. Mugs was there. We nodded politely at each other. What would I say: "Hey, remember that time I saw you at the bakery?" Mugs just about fit in. He had on the right clothes—a bit more worn than those of his would-be peers—but clean, casually rakish. But I sensed a difference between him and the people in that crowd. It had to do with a certain indefinable leanness or readiness, and any further description lapses even further into cliché: the right stuff, the real thing, a hard man. A look more at home there, probably, than anywhere else; shared, even, by a few others. Nonetheless, I wondered if others envied Mugs. The others, those spending fewer and fewer days in the mountains and more days taking care of business? Or was it vice versa? Did they secretly pity Mugs, and might he have envied them?

I had been gone from Olympia only a few months when someone called to tell me that Willi Unsoeld had died in an avalanche on Rainier. In the following weeks, dark and speculative rumors abounded—not the sort to be voiced publicly—about how so-and-so had been to Rainier the day before the accident and pronounced snow conditions to be the worst he had ever seen; about how someone had heard Willi say that this next time up would be his last above ten thousand feet, that his hips wouldn't carry him any longer. Soon people began whispering, "He knew," packing into the two

simple words deep and various meanings, accompanied b
own knowing looks. The truth is, of course, unavailable.

You will often read in tributes to climbers who die in the mun-
tains that "they died doing what they loved." Though no doubt true,
this does not mean that someone who dies climbing dies happily or
chooses to do so. This "died doing what he loved" stuff is post facto
rationalization that we the living engage in to comfort ourselves. I've
joked about death during times it was probably closest. I wouldn't
call it either bravado or false bravado—more that by speaking the
name of the beast, we keep it at arm's length.

Jim Bridwell titled the account of his and Mugs's ascent of the
East Face of the Moose's Tooth "The Dance of the Woo-Li Masters."
There is a lot more truth to the title than Bridwell ever alludes to in
the account. I don't just mean the dancing part. We all know the Wil-
liam Butler Yeats poem (okay, perhaps not the poem, but the concept at least) asking how we can tell the dancer from the dance. That
question rings especially true when the dancer is gone, and only a
trace of the dance remains.

Wu li is a Chinese term that means, roughly, patterns of energy,
or physics. But since *wu* also means seventy-nine other things, depending on how it's pronounced, interpretation is considerably
more complicated. In his explanation of the new physics, *The Dancing Wu Li Masters*, Gary Zukav gives the five essential meanings
of *wu li*: Patterns of Energy, My Way, Nonsense (*wu* as nonbeing or
void), I Clutch My Ideas, and Enlightenment. They sound like chap-
ters in an expedition account or a climber's biography.

But it is with *masters* that Bridwell has struck a chord. "Whatever
he [the Master] does," writes Zukav, "he does it with the enthusiasm
of doing it for the first time. This is the source of his unlimited energy." So must it have been for Mugs. How else could he climb the
Supercouloir on Fitz Roy, the East Face of the Moose's Tooth, and
the North Buttress of Mount Hunter in a single year? How else could
he solo the Cassin over ten years later, entering the fifth decade of
his life?

If Albert Einstein had been a climber, I doubt he would have said, "God does not play dice with the universe." Rather he would have often seen the dice rolling. How else can we make sense out of Bridwell and Mugs's being able to rap off a single number 3 Stopper on one day and on another day for the mountain to move under Mugs's feet? So the dice roll.

When we start out climbing, we are looking for something. We do not know what exactly that something is, but we know we will recognize it when we find it. When we do find it, we are still relatively inarticulate about what we have found. We know that we want to find it again, bask in that moment. There is a very real sense in which these moments defy the ability of language to capture them. Peter Croft described an example of this phenomenon in his recent slide show. He said that when he sees the friends he was with on an expedition to Nepal, they don't even really talk to each other; they just sit around grinning at one another.

Mugs must have had a lot to smile about. He describes a night just below the top of Hunter's North Buttress: "I thought of what I'd done to get here, not just in the last four days, but in years past. For some reason, I felt part of some great movement, one of infinite scale, too grand to see but only to feel in the night's wind." There is a lot of the transcendent in climbing. We don't talk much about it, not only because we're not good enough with words, though that's part of our relative silence. It's understood: to speak publicly about it is—I don't know—unbecoming. Transcendence and death, ever present in climbing: we don't talk about them until we have to.

The poet Elizabeth Bishop asks, "Oh, must we dream our dreams and have them, too?" It's a plaintive cry, and a cautionary rhetorical question. We should be careful what we wish for; sometimes wishing alone may suffice. Which brings me back to Gatsby. He made a couple mistakes: he thought the ideal could be made real, and he thought you could repeat the past. Nick, the guy who tells the story, is pretty much an observer of the events he writes about: the only thing he ever really does besides tell the story is tell Gatsby that he's "worth the whole damn bunch put together." Mugs dreamed the dream and had it, made the ideal climb reality, and repeated the past many times by climbing at the jagged, wavering edge of the abyss for so long. We love our heroes, but we're damned hard on them. We admire them for making the choices we quite deliberately did not make. That day in the bakery, I was far short of telling Mugs that he was worth the whole damn bunch put together—too unbecoming. But I think it's true; I'm saying it now.

1993

I stop by Mugs's marker in the Talkeetna cemetery about once a year. His body, of course, has never been recovered. How many times since his passing have I (we) said, "Not X, of all people"? Some people make mistakes in the mountains and are never called to account for them. Others do everything "right," and it's lights out. For many of the climbers I have known who lost their lives in the mountains, their single biggest mistake was being there in the first place. As Edward Whymper warned in *Scrambles amongst the Alps* back in 1865: "Climb if you will, but remember that courage and strength are naught without prudence, and that a momentary negligence may destroy the happiness of a lifetime. Do nothing in haste; look well to each step; and from the beginning think what may be the end."

VIRGA

Along the bleached shores of Mono Lake, thousands of
breeding gulls scavenge bits and pieces of this and that
for their nests. This full juju is defined in the dictionary
as good luck, but only the gull knows the reason behind
collecting its booty of fishing gear, colorful plastics, and
ribbons. The gulls frequent the dump, picnic areas, and
local restaurants for these decorative nest treasures.

—From a display at the Mono Lake Visitor Center

First we follow directions: twenty miles on the Benton Crossing
Road. Forty minutes and no signs of humanity later, the crags come
into view. Another mile and a half up a steep, deeply rutted dirt
road. From here the view is impressive: of nothing—an unnamed
mountain range and back to Benton Crossing Road, where no cars
tread. But now tire tracks, a firepit. The tribe has been here.

We stagger up to the crags, panting thickly in the thin eight-
thousand-foot air. The guidebook drawing is crudely made, poorly
reproduced, barely readable. Although the climbs are named and
listed in order, they are utterly indistinguishable from one another:
Jimmy Jones, Caligula, Psycho Killer, Psycho Chicken, Mayhem,
Hillside Strangler.

We locate what we think is a distinct line, although from below
we have no idea where it goes at the top.

I find a hawk feather.

We are being bitten mercilessly by small flies.

We do the climb, which comes highly recommended with three asterisks that we understand to be stars: a three-star route. Adventurous. From the top we make a short rappel and then a scary down-climb on slabs.

We find another climb, easier than the first, leading to a spacious, comfy alcove high on the rock overlooking the empty valley. The clumps of high cumulus have darkened and are loosing rain into the air. It is *virga*, the rain that falls toward the high desert but never reaches the ground. From the top of this one we can walk off fearlessly.

For lunch, smoked cheddar on sourdough and Cloud 9 chocolate, dark and pocked with raspberries. We split an orange and wash it down with icy cold water.

Perhaps one more climb. We wander around the rock formations; there are four or five of them rising like castles out of the hillside. Eventually we reach the last formation, which finally gives us a sense of having found our bearings. There in the sand I see a Black Diamond carabiner, better than any I own.

"A sign!" I say.

"Of what?" says Jim.

"That I've found a carabiner."

Instantly I feel foolish. For a moment I had been in my meaning-making mode, caught up in the desire for things—that is objects, events, coincidences, the natural world—to mean more than they are. But then I returned intuitively (this formalization in language coming later) to the poet's dictum: insistence upon the thing itself. In climbing, the safest operating principle is to assume that a thing is what it is. I once heard a talk by Christopher Isherwood, whose lesser-known works include the play *The Ascent of F6*, a 1930s collaboration with W. H. Auden, which foresaw much of the folly surrounding today's overblown mountaineering expeditions. Isherwood told a story about D. H. Lawrence's seeing a fish on the shore and saying, "Look, the symbol of Christian faith and fellowship!" And Isherwood said, "Yes, and life was never boring again."

A hawk feather is just a hawk feather, even if for a moment one wishes, as if the thing itself were not enough, to make something more of it.

We locate a many-asterisked route, although we are unsure of the start, and high above I can clearly see two impossible sections. Also, I am tired. Weary. Unfortunately, my wrist—so sore the previous night that I could not twist the cap off a Sierra Nevada Pale Ale—is not feeling bad right now. A damned shame too, as I actually injured it climbing, therefore potentially providing an honorable excuse to wuss out.

But no, Jim has a vision and is racking the gear. Putting on a climbing harness, after years of climbing, becomes second nature. But perhaps for precisely this reason people do it sloppily—forgetting to double back the loose end of the waist belt—the equivalent of missing a loop when putting on a belt with jeans, but with far more serious consequences. The act must be deliberate. Sometimes when my wife and I are working with our children, we say, "It's your decision," meaning something like "We think we've given you the tools to construct what we see as the right decision." They choose what we think of as wrong often enough, but we imagine they are learning to take responsibility for their actions.

I know my wife sees climbing as somehow irresponsible: at least an activity that takes me away from the family, at worst one that puts me in danger. For what? she'd like to know. As I twist the rope into a figure-8 knot and loop it through and back on itself, I imagine her saying, "It's your decision." And I act deliberately.

Jim acts even more deliberately, leading up awkwardly, stopping ninety or a hundred feet above to bring me up. I follow nimbly—the adverb applying to a climbing style that tends to be possible only when the rope is above me. When the rope is above you, falling is "no worries, man." Lead climbing is another story. When you're leading, your end of the rope is called the "sharp end." The clouds, as I climb, gather in thick, menacing bunches.

From where I meet Jim, I can see that the second pitch still seems to hold unclimbable passages as well as unprotectable ones (meaning that if you're the leader and you fall, you may well die). Above us a squawking group of seagulls swoops and wheels around, in seeming imitation of raptors or larger scavengers. They're far from the Pacific and far from Mono Lake, their traditional breeding grounds, far in fact from any water at all except that which is about to drop out of the sky.

"What are they doing here?" Jim asks.

It's not an unreasonable question. I'm a naturalist working in the area; I know a few things. But I have to shrug. "They're confused," I say.

"Lot of that going around," he says.

Jim smoothly leads through all problems but the last. Here he hesitates, then superhumanly disappears from view, over the lip of the impossible. Now it is beginning to rain. My goal is to climb quickly to the final impossible moves before a downpour occurs, and to dangle there until Jim pulls me over the top or I die of hypothermia. I'm dramatizing: the first scenario truly impossible—one person can't really pull another up a sheer face; and the second, hypothermia, is unlikely though not impossible.

I do arrive at the crux before a downpour occurs, but the moves are still impossible. For ten minutes I stand there on footholds the size of fifty-cent pieces (it would be a gross exaggeration to call them dime-sized, the climber's stock metaphor, or to imply that I'm hanging off their edges by my fingernails). I am thinking about the difficulties, and then I calmly surmount them, as if detached. Whatever has just happened, it has nothing to do with brute force nor force of will. A few feet up, I am sitting in a large pothole watching the thunderstorm close the gap between the unnamed ridge and us.

The hail hits as we're setting up the rappel off a natural horn of rock on the back side. I'm thinking of my splendid high-tech jacket purchased just a week earlier with birthday money from my parents. The jacket is in the car. We are wearing cotton T-shirts. Today is my birthday.

We toss the rope out, and because there's an overhang below us, we can't know for sure if it reaches the bottom. We know it's close. With the rope stretching, it will reach, we tell ourselves. People die fairly often by rappelling off the ends of their ropes. In climbing there are many ways, most of them literal, to be at the end of one's rope. But death seems unlikely here. And it's raining.

The rappel is smooth and surprisingly airy—free, it's called— with the rope hanging over an edge, the climber spinning in the air. The rope reaches the ground as if cut to size. And it drops us into a slot of perhaps ten feet between the rock we have just descended and another of the castle-like formations. The rain is falling harder now, but we're on the ground, where nothing very bad can befall us, or so we tell ourselves. One summer I did a long climb in Alaska and returned in a state of shock, paralyzed by a retrospective fear of the potential for disaster, until I was in a car accident that winter: the real danger, I realized, was everywhere.

Now, there can't be more than a half hour between us and the car, and we feel the warmth generated by having just done something with an uncertain outcome.

We skirt around the base of the formation, back to the beginning of the climb where we left our packs. In a moment of atypical efficiency I had tucked Jim's camera and guidebook into his pack and covered my hiking shoes with my own pack. As I rounded a final corner, those nylon things of the world came back into view.

The hail pelts us and we laugh, like, "Can you believe this?" This is the laugh of those who know that the car, replete with chocolate and beer, is no more than fifteen minutes away. Reading the journals of John Cheever—a harrowing record of domestic unhappiness—I found the surprising and uplifting lines: "I do not seek it for long, but how wonderful it is to see at last a vision of wholeness, including some mountains." My friend John Boe found this hilarious considering the source: "Yes," he said, "Cheever in the mountains. Preferably seen from one's sofa with a gin and tonic in hand."

Then amid the loud patter, something more furious than patter really, hard rain and hail, a faint clink and "Damn," says Jim, "My wedding ring." For luck he wears it around his neck when we climb. Its string has broken.

Which reminds me of how hard our route had been: Jim said "fuck" twice during the climb. In our sixteen years of climbing together I've heard him utter the word perhaps only a half-dozen times. In such situations as leading onto dicey ground or losing my wedding ring, my personal mantra, informed by years of study and acquired sensitivity to the subtleties of language, is a string of expletives worthy of a street thug in a drug deal gone bad. Now Jim has lost his wedding ring in a hailstorm in the mountains, and all he says is "damn." Jim is a mathematician. Sometimes I think climbing is all we have in common.

"Don't worry," I say, "we'll stay until we find it." All magnanimous and giddy am I, not wanting any mundane misfortune to take the edge off the climb.

Now the rain is sluicing off the rock, forming pools on the ground, waterfalls everywhere, and we are on our hands and knees raking through the twigs and rocks, pine needles, and volcanic sand. Five minutes.

We expand the search slightly: Nothing. We can't believe it. Ten minutes.

"I was right here when I heard it hit the rocks," he says. Our clothes are now soaked.

I take my eyes off the ground and look at him. "The cuffs of your pants," I say. "Let me check." And there it is.

This puts a final sweet spin on events, and I'm feeling lucky, I'm finding stuff, my mojo's rising, baby. The Nevada border is only about five miles to the east on the road to Hawthorne. We could be there in a heartbeat, and I could let a twenty ride on the roulette wheel at a strong contender for the much-contested crown of Nevada's ugliest casino slash truckstop slash whorehouse slash trailer park. But I've been paying enough attention to know it's not that kind of mojo.

It continues to rain as we traipse to the car. And I think now of "the walk to the car" as a discrete concept or event, and of one time at Peshastin Pinnacles more than twenty years ago, Roy and I walking though an apple orchard, sprinklers soaking us with thick cords of water, and we just didn't care. Nothing could touch us. In another world, a relentless stream of bills amasses in the post office box, and more ambitious assistant professors everywhere slouch toward tenure. Fuck it, I think, I'm forty-four today.

Now, the car windows steamed by our wet clothes and body heat, we drive homeward out of the rain. Tomorrow, Charlie, who's lived here for over forty years (but is still not considered a local by the locals), will say, "Some road, isn't it?" and I will agree. "The only people who went out there," he says, "were the lionhunters." *Lionhunters*, he says, all one word. "But now," he adds, "No one goes out there."

Later, some weeks after the climbing, one of the summer's minor disasters occurs, one we all laugh about now in hindsight: the family gondola ride to the top of Mammoth Mountain. Our four-year-old son became terrified the moment the gondola swung free of the loading dock. His fear was so abject, so palpable, that we couldn't be angry with him, only sympathetic. Once we reached the top, this fear was unabated: we set off to walk down the road, and he feared we would fall off it, even though there was no place to fall. He was like a cow spooked by one of those fake cattle guards painted yellow on the blacktop. We had no choice but to get back on the gondola and descend immediately. Once back on the ground, our older son, a worldly six years old, to our surprise, emptied his pockets. We hadn't been anywhere long enough to fill his pockets, nor had we witnessed it, nonetheless here were

> a wrapper from a candy bar;
> a grommet with a twist of yellow rope knotted to it;
> a stick;
> a couple lift-ticket wires;

a strand of orange nylon baling twine;

a basket from a ski pole;

two small rocks, neither possessing a single
distinguishable feature.

"What's this stuff?" I asked—and what I really meant was "When did you pick up all this crap?" It was all covered, by the way, with a thick layer of dust.

He looked at me as if of all the stupid questions I had ever asked (and there have been many), this had to be the stupidest.

"Treasure," he said.

1997

This was written after the second summer (1997) that I worked for the Inyo National Forest at the Mono Lake Visitor Center. The best thing about these three summers was that we had our young sons there with us, and they could learn something of the larger world beyond the cornfields of rural Illinois. The second best thing was that the fate of Mono Lake was turning into a small victory for the environment, with a court mandate restoring the flow of freshwater into the saline, terminal, and shrinking lake.

This is one of the few pieces of writing here that feature my partnership with Jim Pinter-Lucke. This is a weirdly disproportionate fact because Jim and I did a lot of climbing together and were perfectly matched partners, trading leads mostly on rock climbs in the Sierra, but also in the Cordillera Blanca in Peru on Alpamayo, a figurative and literal high point for both of us.

UNTETHERED
IN YOSEMITE

A Report from Paradise in the
Last Summer of the Millennium

QUESTION ASKED OF EUROPEAN SPORT CLIMBERS:
"Would you ever consider going to Yosemite and trying
some crack classics like Phoenix, Alien, or Cosmic Debris?"

ANSWER: If it's on our way we might. These are classics
after all, though, no good for training purposes. Where is
Yosemite, by the way?

I do not expect in this lifetime to be bored by Yosemite Valley, or
ever to tire of driving eastward through the Wawona Tunnel. That
first glimpse of El Capitan from the car window has never failed to
lift my spirits, to give me an almost visceral thrill, to humble me.
That is why, I suppose, I so admire those who never leave. I don't
believe they stay because they have no other options, no sense of
the larger world outside the Valley, nothing else to which they are so
well suited. Though all these may also be true, I believe they are sec-
ondary to the certain knowledge that for these people, Yosemite is
unmatched. "This is the place," they say in effect, as Brigham Young
is said to have said at the physical end of a spiritual journey.

Perhaps for its indigenous peoples Yosemite was an Eden, but we can't know exactly what they thought, Eden being an Old World concept and the record of mid-nineteenth-century Miwok culture secondhand and sketchy at best. In the first written description of the Valley, *Discovery of Yosemite and the Indian War of 1851 Which Led to That Event*, Lafayette Bunnell describes almost simultaneously the holy beauty of the place and the vanquishing of the first peoples who lived there. This historical moment is a very precise example of Renato Rosaldo's notion of "imperialist nostalgia," as described in *Culture and Truth*: "The phenomenon of mourning what one has destroyed."

When Yosemite is referred to as edenic today, I think it is often done with the design of disproving the notion. David Robertson, in his introduction to *West of Eden: A History of the Art and Literature of Yosemite*, delineates this point nicely: "The wilderness areas of America are, of course, quite different from Eden. . . . Yet our journey to the wilderness may, at a deep and even partly unconscious level, be a peculiarly American way of seeking paradise." For the rock climber, despite recent trends that value speed and technical difficulty over style and a sense of adventure, Yosemite remains an unparalleled paradise.

I spent the summer of 1999 on the east side of the Sierra, in the small mountain town of Lee Vining, just down from Tioga Pass, the eastern entrance to Yosemite National Park. In describing the place to those with no concept of where it might be, I always say, "Just east of Yosemite," the way I might have said "Detroit" years ago when asked where I was from, when in truth it was the suburbs west of the city. After this summer they will say: "Yosemite, hey! Where that woman got her head chopped off?" "Yeah," I admit. It happened about thirty miles away as the crow flies, but I think by the time I heard about it they had caught the guy. I felt bad for the victim, of course, but I also felt that a sacred space, a spiritual refuge, had been violated. I learned in tenth-grade biology class that too many rats in the terrarium lead to aberrant behavior. As the Yosemite National Park literature warns us, the Valley receives four million visitors per year, most concentrated in the two or so square miles of the valley floor, although the park itself occupies 1,200 square miles of largely undeveloped landscape.

In her book on the American West, *Savage Dreams*, Rebecca Solnit reexamines the etymology of the name Yosemite, finding that it means probably not "grizzly," as long thought, but "some among them are killers." Ironically, it was the white settlers who named the place with a Miwok word, despite the fact that they, the white men, were the killers. The Miwok were expelled from their valley homeland of nearly a millennium by the Mariposa Battalion, which included Lafayette Bunnell. Francis P. Farquhar, author of *History of the Sierra Nevada,* reports that Chief Tenaya, who saw his son brutally murdered by the whites, prophesied and threatened: "Yes, sir, American, my spirit will make trouble for you and your people, as you have caused trouble for me and my people." And, indeed there are some killers in the Valley today. I've always thought stupidity, gravity, and bad judgment to be the top three, but I suppose we can now add psycho killer to the list.

Early in June I'm climbing up the southeast slope—the easy route—of Mount Morrison. Morrison is east and south of Yosemite, just off Highway 395. I'm alone—it is, after all, the easy route. A few miles in and I can feel a blister forming on my heel, probably a large one.

I sit on a rock looking up into the basin below Mount McAddie—a wild, unvisited place just a few miles from the highway. My foot will be wrecked if I continue; I'm still at the beginning of a long day, yet I don't seriously consider turning back.

I just want to be up there. That choice to continue seems significant somehow, or maybe what's significant is that it didn't even come to being a choice. And for a while—the rest of the day—I feel *untethered.*

The climb is not quite so easy as I thought it would be: it's completely covered in snow and steep in parts. But it's also shorter than

I had imagined, and soon I'm up there with the whole glorious panorama of the Sierra to myself. I can see north past Mono Lake toward Reno, east across Nevada, south to dozens and dozens of giant Sierra peaks whose individuality is subsumed by a sense of totality: granite, snow, and blue sky forever and ever. I feel giddy—as Ralph Waldo Emerson had it, "glad to the brink of fear." I take a lot of photographs, knowing as I snap them off that they will bore anyone but me. I write mushy, sentimental stuff in the summit register—words I would surely disown at sea level. And I return, thinking of those who choose to stay untethered, not for an afternoon, or a weekend or a summer, but past the point of no return. Out there, up there.

In Yosemite valley at the base of Nutcracker: the line, or the queue, as the Aussie kid would have it. He and his partner, Tom, are just ahead of us. Ahead of them are two Japanese couples and three guys just starting up, nine climbers in all: if solitude and wilderness are inextricably linked in our minds, this day will offer neither. Nutcracker is a moderate Yosemite classic with historic significance. Royal Robbins put the route up in the sixties without using any pitons for protection—a revolutionary act at the time. The line of climbers is expected. Tom has taken off his shirt and spread out his gear on it, apparently immune to the mosquitoes. In two previous attempts on Nutcracker, I've given in to heat and fear in varying proportions. This day the weather is perfect, the hour not too late. We will wait.

Then the leader of the three-person team backs off, is lowered down the wall. His friend goes up, only to take a thirty-foot fall that leaves him much bloodied and shaken, but otherwise miraculously unhurt. For a while this does not deter them, and they plan to reattack, but soon good judgment prevails, and the bleeding man goes for medical help. They ask if we would please retrieve their gear, left at their high point. Of course. Four of the others start up a variation, and suddenly it's our turn. It has been agreed (but not aloud) that my partner, Jim, will be taking the hard leads. I believe this intuitive shared knowledge is based on the fact that I now live in the Midwest, that my children are young, that my waistline is expanding—the usual excuses. This day marks twenty years since the first time Jim and I roped up together.

The climb is as advertised, a classic, the weather a dream. Even the other people, the waiting, do not interfere with our pleasure. The crux moves are hard, as advertised, but soon we are on the summit, having overcome a surprising stretch of unprotected terrain near the top. The summit block, too, is a dream, with its spectacular views of the Cathedral group to the west and Half Dome looming above us to the east. Despite the day's share of the four million visitors who drive through the valley each year, soon to be standing in lines for cabin reservations, ice cream cones, and T-shirts exhorting "Go Climb a Rock," and despite the many climbers on the route, we have the summit all to ourselves. You can walk off this one more or less hassle-free. All in all, we got what we wanted out of the day, though it's hard always to say exactly what that is.

As a Forest Service employee on the east side, I read the Yosemite National Park public news bulletins that are faxed to us daily. There is an important difference between national parks and national forests: parks are operated basically like museums, in effect, preserved; forests are operated more like a business with a multiple-use mandate. Recreation is one use of the forest, but not the one that pays the bills: mining, grazing, and logging rights on national forest lands bring in millions of dollars for the federal government. The budget for operating the forests, however, is doled out by Congress and seems to bear no logical, much less financial, connection to the monies that the forest takes in.

The first Yosemite news bulletin that catches my eye this summer is about the BASE jumper who landed safely after leaping off El Cap, ran from rangers waiting to arrest him, thumbed his nose at them, and leapt into the raging Merced River. BASE stands for buildings, antennae, spans, and earth, the fixed objects from which these skydivers leap. Robbie Slater, before he was killed descending from the summit of K2, had done the exact same thing, leaping off El Cap and escaping by way of the river. This season's BASE jumper, however, has not been seen since—an outlaw, the stuff of legends.

The second news bulletin out of Yosemite announced the rock slide on the Glacier Point Apron. The Apron is a huge slab of granite that rises from just south of Curry Village, site of one of the largest concentrations of humanity within the park. The US Geological Survey estimated the rockfall at about 525 tons. In a strange twist, a climber died while belaying, but his friends above him survived. Accidents of geology seem closest to the hand of God, do they not? According to the USGS, these rocks have been exposed to weathering for more than the last one million years. If your number's up, your number's up, right?

Yosemite Search and Rescue has a spotting scope set up in the Curry Village parking lot. Watching the cracks in the rocks expand, watching geology. I mention to the spotter that the story of the climber's death as reported in the *Los Angeles Times* was hard to visualize. "Hey," he said, "its purpose wasn't for you to visualize it. Whatever you can say to make the family feel better. Why say anything else?" Then, in response to the question he was doubtless tired of hearing: "Gravity's the same today as it was yesterday. Rock will fall, but you can't say when."

Late in the afternoon after our climb of Nutcracker, Jim and I are wandering around the tourist sites, stopping regularly to rehydrate, taking in the scene. Jim calls his wife, and there at the phone booth next to him is Ron Kauk. Moments earlier I had contemplated purchasing a poster of Kauk on a climbing route called Peace, rated 5.13c on a difficulty scale whose limit was 5.9 when originally designed. The route is in in Tuolumne Meadows, almost six thousand vertical feet above the valley floor. Kauk had made the first free ascent of Astroman (the East Face of Washington Column) and of Midnight Lightning, the world's most famous bouldering problem, in Camp 4. I saw him climb in the World Sport Climbing Championship at Snowbird when I lived in Salt Lake City.

Most of us were at the competition to see the French phenom of the day, Patrick Edlinger, and I suppose technically speaking he was the best. But when Kauk climbed, there was an electric hushing of the crowd. It might have been that his presence hadn't been expected, or that unlike all the rest, he did not wear Lycra tights. It might, too, have been that he was an American—Native American, in fact. But I think it was something else, something intangible. It had to do with fluidity and grace, with the only real kind of style, acquired by aspiring to no style. *Aspiring* is not even the right word; a more Zen-like verb is required. What emanated from Kauk had everything to do with climbing and nothing to do with competition. When he popped off near the top of the final overhang, he had somehow nonetheless given us a vision of how it might be done.

And now here he was talking into a pay phone, and then sitting back down at a table of friends.

He looks like an ordinary person, except, I suppose, better looking. In any other American endeavor, a person of his stature probably would be sitting in the leather seats of a BMW talking on a cellular phone. There can be no doubt that he pays a high price for his life as he lives it.

That night in Camp 4 we see the Japanese from Nutcracker: filterless cigarettes all around, and two one-gallon bottles of Canadian Club on the picnic table. Camp 4 is now officially called Sunnyside Walk-In Campground. Three tents to a site, no reservations, fourteen-day limit. The name Camp 4 is a remnant of the 1960s, the golden age of Yosemite climbing. Most of the occupants are climbers, and it's packed. It's hard, on this day impossible, to get a campsite in midsummer. We're on our way to site 19, where two guys said we could sleep in their tent while they did a high bivy to get an early start on Snake Dike, the easiest climbing route on Half Dome. At site 19 there are six tents. We don't even know the guys' names—they were behind us on Nutcracker. A person appears and directs us to the tent we're looking for. I would be remiss here if I did not mention that this person was a dwarf.

We then go to site 26 to return the gear left by the guys who fell on Nutcracker. Then across the road to the Mountain Room Bar, which is devoid of climbers and filled with people watching the NBA finals, eyes glued to the two TVs. Here is the difference, I think: these people *are* tethered to this world. A couple days later I'm back at work on the east side, thinking about going to the Tiger Bar down in June Lake to watch a basketball game myself. Alan, a firefighter who lives a few cabins over, says, "It's the finals?"

"Yep." It's not a comfortable role, serving as Alan's connection to world news.

"Who's playing?"

I tell him, and he looks at me in disbelief. "Shee—oot," he says. "Are we still in Kosovo?" (We are.)

He shakes his head and laughs at himself and/or the larger forgotten world.

The next morning I am up early in Camp 4. A familiar-looking man in running shorts—he looks like a Euro (what is that look, anyway?) but is coming from the Search and Rescue tents. The muscles in his legs are those of a world-class athlete. Wind- and sunburned. Hard.

An hour later he's drinking coffee in the lounge, and I realize suddenly he's Werner Braun. About ten years ago he had climbed Astroman over fifty times. I remember the first time seeing his name and thinking von Braun, the rocket man. But this man is Braun, and the climb is Astroman.

I can't describe Astroman to you very well. It has a climbing pedigree rarely matched. Originally called the East Face of Washington Column, it was first climbed in 1959 by the Yosemite climbing pioneers Warren Harding, Glen Denny, and Chuck Pratt. All three were significant figures in the climbing world. This was an aid climb, meaning that climbers were "aided" by hanging directly from their gear. During the climb, which was accomplished over a long period, Steve Roper ferried water up fixed ropes to the climbers and took photos that were published, by Harding's prior arrangement, in the *Oakland Tribune*. This was the first money—thirty dollars—Roper made from climbing; later he would write the first climbers' guidebook to Yosemite.

The first free ascent of the same route was made by climbers from the next generation—John Bachar, John Long, and Ron Kauk in 1975. A free ascent is a climb made in a purer style. No hanging or resting on gear is allowed—hands and feet use holds on the rock only. They rechristened the route Astroman. It's rated 5.11c, considerably more difficult than anything I have ever done.

I was telling the story of seeing Werner Braun to young Sean, a first-time visitor to the Sierra and an accomplished climber. That is, he had done some hard sport routes at Smith Rock up in Oregon. He didn't know of Braun or Astroman.

"Have you done it?" he asked me, referring to Astroman.

I laughed. "No."

"Are you going to do it?"

"No," I said. And I remembered the day I knew I wouldn't do Astroman (which would have been any day I had given it any thought). Bob Schneider and I—Bob who had actually done it years earlier, when it was an aid climb—were talking in the indoor climbing gym. Some climbs recede from you, others you can keep in sight out there on the horizon. Two guys in their forties, climbing in a gym. No, we would never do Astroman.

But this concept was lost on the youth, Sean, to whom everything was still possible.

I wonder about Werner Braun's count today, if he even keeps count.

In the George Myers and Don Reid guidebook—the most comprehensive of the guidebooks, listing over six hundred routes in the Valley—a note after Astroman says, "This is the free climb." I had always read this to mean that this is *the* free climb. But I suppose the note is there to distinguish it from the aid climb. In *Yosemite Select*, a shorter guidebook of only the classics, Reid says it's "probably the best free climb in the Valley." And if it's the best free climb in the Valley, for many, it has to be the best in the world. One imagines Werner saying to himself, It simply can't get any better than this, therefore, I will continue to do this route over and over and over.

News bulletin number 3: early in June a hiker loses his footing in the river and is shot over Nevada Falls, a 492-foot drop to the valley floor. A multitude of signs in several languages warns against doing exactly what he did. How could someone do this stupid thing? Could it be that here the danger the signs warn us of is so literal, so immediate, and that elsewhere it's not? That the other warnings cluttering our lives are crying wolf too loudly, too often? There are warnings and there are *warnings*, right? This happens nearly every summer.

Jim and I drive up to Tuolumne Meadows. The Italians are behind us on a route called South Crack above Tenaya Lake. Their leader overlaps us at belay stations, a cheerful fellow singing Neil Diamond songs in Italian. He wishes to know if Budweiser is the best American beer. Is there any climbing in Chicago? There's really only one word of English he understands perfectly: *runout*. The word refers to expanses of rock which the leader cannot protect; he risks a long and serious fall should he lose his grip or footing. Tuolumne climbs are known for runout routes, and South Crack is one of them. The Italian sings out randomly, trilling the r: *rrrunout!*

I tell Jim about the first time I did South Crack. That time, a man appeared behind me, silently. It was a surprise because usually you can hear the clanking and tinkling of climbing hardware. He climbed through, passing me. He was soloing, which is why I didn't hear his gear jangling—he had none. We're about four or five hundred feet off the deck. All I can think to say to him is, "How many times have you done this route?"

"I don't know," he says. "About two hundred."

Untethered.

At the top Jim and I see a man in a red hat. He's yelling, "Down!" and waving wildly. A crazy Euro-tourist, we figure, *down* his only word of English. Soloed something in his driving moccasins, no doubt, and now doesn't know how to get down.

"Down!" he yells.

We are above and beyond him by a couple hundred yards, on the long, slow road down, following cairns and dirt paths.

When we get back to the car, there's the guy in the red hat. He was trying to show us the fastest way down, he says. We laugh, having thought it was he who was asking us how to get down.

No, he says, he used to guide here. That was the way he took clients down.

It's a small world and I suddenly realize to whom we're speaking: "T. M. Herbert?" I venture.

"Yes," he says.

In Yosemite the golden age is recent enough that the gods mingle casually with mortals, as if they were not gods at all. I know my history.

Herbert, whose son Tommy is a world-class rock climber as well, says he stopped soloing South Crack the previous year. Too old, he says—it's sensible to stop soloing 5.8. Hard to disagree with that.

He's sixty-three.

Figures he's done South Crack 250 times, and Great White Book, the route he'd soloed today, about 500.

The Italians in their Speedos are lying out on flat rocks on the edge of Tenaya Lake.

Once at this very spot, Kathy Roper sat reading a book at the lakeshore while her husband Steve and I climbed a short route on the rock above. Day hikers paused to watch a bear roam the opposite shore. A tourist remarked to Kathy that he'd seen "trout, bears, and idiots," nodding upward in our direction.

I enjoy being in Yosemite with my children. They like to swim, hike, and climb on the boulders. I see a different Yosemite when I'm with them, and it's a bit more populated, yes, but it's beautiful, too. My youngest, Macklin, looks closely at the world, but his gaze is usually directed toward the ground: things that are small, things that crawl, things that are camouflaged. He sees all these with the eyes of a young animal. But he doesn't often know where he is, quite, in the larger scheme. Look up there, I say, Yosemite Falls just having come into view. He directs his gaze to the sky, and there they are: the falls.

"Holy crap," he whispers.

Later, at the scene of writing, Macklin approaches me: "What are you doing?"

"Writing." I am not inviting further inquiry. In fact, writing is something I almost never attempt when my children are in the house, i.e., all the time I'm at home.

"Oh," he says. "Is it about me?"

Strange enough that I actually was writing, stranger still that I was, in fact, writing about him. I read the previous paragraph aloud to him. An expression of deep concern overcomes him.

"What?" I ask.

"Not good," he says. Now I invite further comment: "What should I be writing?"

"Say that at Yosemite a UFO came down and took Macklin away. They'll like that."

Whenever I swim with my children at the Curry Village pool in the Valley I can't help taking a few minutes to sit in the shallow end and look north to the Royal Arches, remembering its classic features: the Pendulum, the long-lost Rotten Log, the Jungle. Today, with large sections of Curry Village fenced off because of the rockslide danger, I'm looking over my shoulder too, back and up at the Apron, thinking about gravity, rockfall, luck, geologic time.

But most of the time I'm watching my kids, to the extent that the lifeguard mentions that he appreciates it that I'm watching them so carefully. I'm glad he's here, of course, but they're *my* kids. Somehow we get onto the topic of the BASE jumper. It's the lifeguard's opinion that his body completely disintegrated in the Merced River, thrashed to atoms against the rocks and logs at peak runoff season. I hadn't considered that: I thought he had simply escaped. If the truth is in between, he's drowned, his body wedged in some lonely high-water place. Of course that's it, I think. Still, I much prefer my version.

Later in the summer I am at Mirror Lake with my family: wife and two boys, six and eight years old. The hike to Mirror Lake is short, the trail is paved, and you can take a bus—for free—halfway there from Curry Village. Hence there are lots of people there; families abound, frat boys at a bachelor party, folks on rented mountain bikes. This is the farthest east in the Valley I've ever been, and here below Half Dome the approach to the climbing routes on the Northwest Face looks as unappealing as I've always heard it to be: loose and dirty rock, steep, slabby, long. Suddenly two guys with mega-loaded packs—including a battered white Fish pack, an esoteric design used exclusively by big wall climbers for gear hauling—appear. They shed their loads slowly—as one must with a hundred-plus pounds of stuff—and sit on the sand. They begin to take their shoes off to cross the river. There's a slow-motion aspect to their actions.

I'm wondering why they'd be coming down this way—the standard descent off the top is down the hiking trail on the other side. So I ask. A traverse, they say, we've done a traverse. Nine days on the wall, twelve nights total, plus another trip up to retrieve gear. They ask if I climb.

I'm hesitant to say yes, because compared to them I'm really just fooling around. I say yes, but so they don't get the wrong idea, add that I've never slept on a portaledge.

They look better than I'd feel if I were them, although their hands look hammered—swollen like sausages is the standard climber's cliché. I mention that, but they don't seem to notice. Later my wife will say they had a look on their faces that she couldn't quite describe. I recognize it, though.

Later on the hike down I catch up to them, and we talk climbing. At first I feel like I'm intruding on private space, mythic ritual: the end of the hike out, the return to the world. We talk about the ice climbing in Lee Vining, the *American Alpine Journal*, the Bugaboos. My son Macklin is delighted with Jay's advice: if we go to the Bugaboos, be sure to cover the tires and hoses of the car with chicken wire so the porcupines won't eat them—exactly the kind of advice a six-year-old expects will be helpful in this world. Without gushing, I try to express the extent of my admiration for what they've just done. Only very late in the conversation did they admit it was a first ascent. A superb achievement—but the world that understands the significance of that is very small. All too soon their climb will become (for everyone but them) a line on a photograph, a few words on a page. I ask if they've named it, but no, they haven't got around to that yet.

Later still, I'll realize that I had met Jay before (I'll also remember that, in another life, I had in fact slept on a portaledge, bad memory being one of the necessaries of continuing to climb). I see Jay at the store sitting at a picnic table, a point of stillness among the blur of tourist activity. You might say he was in a daze. But, as I've said, I know the look—seen it in the mirror. He's been untethered, and now he's in between. Exhausted, content, still, at peace, spaced, happy to be alive, to be unburdened of the pack, to be sitting down on a bench, happy to be holding a bottle of beer, feeling the beady coolness of the glass against one's hand, too tired to remember to drink from it.

Could it be that all visitors to Yosemite since (and including) Lafayette Bunnell have been seeking the same thing? The climbers, the tourists, the BASE jumpers, the people watching television in the Mountain Room Bar, the Europeans in their Speedos? David

Robertson has speculated that "perhaps what we seek most in the wilderness is a return to a new and different Eden." Of course, Yosemite's status as wilderness is much in doubt. A small area that receives four million visitors a year cannot really be wilderness. But although some of the climbing routes are crowded, it has always been possible to get away from it all. I have sat on ledges just a few hundred feet off the Valley floor as the sun set and watched its golden light pour through the mouth of the Valley, illuminating the granite walls and spires and glinting off the Merced as if it were a river of mercury. Though I know there are thousands of people below me, they are unseen, swallowed up by the canopy of black oak and lodgepole pine that obscures even most of the buildings and roads. And, somehow—it seems miraculous—there is silence. Something happens. It may be that I have found, as Robertson says, "a natural regeneration and mental and spiritual well-being." But there's something about those words, that language, that I distrust, as if they were not descriptors of experience but a kind of betrayal of it. I'm not sure that language can ever describe this feeling very well, and maybe that too is why I'll keep returning, year after year, to Yosemite, still a paradise, as the third millennium begins.

2000

I am more indebted than my essay might imply to the three books mentioned in the text: David Robertson's *West of Eden,* which makes clear that art always describes a history and shapes a future; Steve Roper's *Camp 4,* which expertly shows how the personal and the historical might be honestly balanced; and Rebecca Solnit's *Savage Dreams: A Journey into the Landscape Wars of the American West,* for its quirky outlook and unflinching historical research. I am also indebted to Scott Slovic's essay "Be Prepared for the Worst: Love, Anticipated Loss, and Environmental Valuation," in *Western American Literature* (Fall 2000), for directing me to Renato Rosaldo's concept of imperialist nostalgia.

Cary Stayner is currently incarcerated on death row in San Quentin Penitentiary for the murder mentioned here and three others near or in Yosemite.

The body of BASE jumper Frank Gambalie III was found pinned beneath a rock in the Merced River twenty-eight days after he was last seen leaping into it. His friend Adam Filipino commented, "They had a freaking serial killer living in Yosemite right under their noses, and federal agents were chasing BASE jumpers to their deaths." It is estimated that about one hundred jumpers a year leap from El Capitan, a Class B misdemeanor that carries a maximum penalty of a five-thousand-dollar fine and six months in jail, and, in most cases, confiscation of the jumper's gear.

Sunnyside Campground, which had been scheduled for demolition to make way for employee housing, has been "saved," largely through a campaign by climbers from around the world. National Park Service Region Director John Reynolds said, "When I heard from climbers from over thirty countries that they hold three places sacred, Everest Basecamp, Chamonix, and Yosemite, I knew we couldn't treat Yosemite like any other climbing area. I knew it was special." Since 2003, Camp 4 has been listed on the National Register of Historic Places.

Current climbing in Yosemite tends toward speed and solo ascents. Alex Honnold and Hans Florine climbed the Nose on El Capitan in 2 hours, 23 minutes, and 46 seconds in 2012 to hold the current record. This is, of course, a mind-boggling achievement. But the element of the unknown has been reduced, so that the only mystery seems to be how fast a route can be climbed. As Peter Croft, the first person to free-solo Astroman (climbing without a rope), has said, "Speed climbing by itself can be a bit of a dead end. It often focuses more on one-upmanship than on mind-expanding grand tours."

Ron Kauk was stunt double for Tom Cruise in the climbing scene that opens *Mission Impossible 2*. Undoubtedly the director had to take great care because Kauk looks so much more like a movie star than Cruise does.

Not long ago, the National Park Service proposed a $386 million plan to, among other things, reduce Valley traffic by building a huge parking lot just west of the park. The Sierra Club is opposed, claiming that no development has ever been good for the park.

Jay Smith and Karl McConachie's route on Half Dome was eventually named Peripheral Vision and was the first complete traverse of the Northwest Face. It involved eighteen full rope lengths of "new ground." In his formal account in the *American Alpine Journal*, Smith called the climb "truly outstanding," adding, "This is a grand tour, especially if you want to see all the routes on the Dome."

Peter Terbush died in the Glacier Point Apron rockslide while heroically belaying his partner. He is memorialized by the Peter Terbush Memorial Summit at Western State Colorado University and by a climb bearing his name in the Black Canyon of Gunnison, Colorado. A wrongful death lawsuit filed by his family was dismissed in 2005.

SHORT WALKS
WITH McINERNEY

Three Classic Pilgrimages

SUPERSTITIOUS

Mont Blanc, French Alps

I'm sitting in the sand on the eastern shore of Lake Michigan. My wife is out shopping, and my children are playing industriously in the dunes. The weather is borderline—cool and threatening rain, not beach weather, but pleasant enough. I am reading Mark Twight's book, *Extreme Alpinism: Climbing Light, Fast, and High.* Among his feats of superalpinism is the Czech Direct, a nine-thousand-foot route on the south face of Denali, that he did with two Übermensch pals in a sixty-hour push. I recall that the first ascent took something like eleven days. I know from Twight's other writings that he is a student of Friedrich Nietzsche and that he hates posers—which is exactly how reading his book makes me feel. It makes a lot of sense, but does not allay my general feeling of unpreparedness about my climbing trip to Chamonix, for which I will depart one day after our family vacation ends.

It's mostly that I simply haven't been climbing enough to be in any kind of shape for climbing. I can run for forty-five minutes in the sand, but how well can that prepare me for a sixteen-hour day on Mont Blanc? I do not need Twight to answer this rhetorical question for me—it's almost universally understood. But Twight makes sense.

Reading him for too long begins to make me nervous, accentuating my general unsuitedness for the tasks at hand. I begin to browse the book, locating the acknowledgments at the end, finding the list of friends (tell 'em you love 'em now) who've died climbing. First on Twight's list is my old friend Dave Kahn, who died somewhat mysteriously on the Dru, a fearsome spire of rock rising out of the Argentière Valley just north of Chamonix—mysteriously in that I have never heard the story at anything like firsthand. I wondered if Twight was Kahn's partner on the climb when he died.

It begins to sprinkle—there aren't many people left on the beach. A man and woman stop their walk directly in front of me; I am maybe twenty-five feet from the shore, and the woman goes in for a swim, the only person in the water. The man turns to watch her, and on the back of his T-shirt is the name KAHN in block letters and the number 00. I resist approaching him and telling him the story of Dave Kahn. The rain picks up, and I gather our things hurriedly, collect the boys, and return to our cabin.

Once there, I realize that in my haste I have lost my reading glasses. Obviously, I just had them: I was reading Twight. I return to the beach in the rain—it's only a few hundred yards—but don't find them, even though there's no real question as to where I was sitting or the route I took back to the cabin. I return again in the fading daylight and repeat the search. The next morning the beach has been scoured flat by the tide, and my glasses are simply gone. No big deal—my insurance will cover another pair. In fact I had already made the optometry appointment. I had recently been to the eye doctor to buy a new pair of sunglasses to wear on the glaciers. A luxury item—I had glasses I could use—but this was a onetime rationalization: take care of your eyes. It's not a luxury to protect your vision at fifteen thousand feet. I went for the iridium-coated

Oakleys, remembering, as I wrote out the check, a line from a student's writing exercise: "Nothing's as pathetic as an old man in a pair of Oakleys."

The next day I take the boys horseback riding. The drive is longer than I recalled, and once we're there, the line is long. I have forgotten the stable's rule about hats: none allowed on the trail—and I return to the car to leave my hat, only to find the keys locked inside. I curse, not too silently, place my hat under the car, and resolve to deal with the situation later.

Once we are on the trail, I realize I'm thinking of nothing but how to get the keys out of the car—specifically, can I get someone to come out and do it on a Sunday afternoon? And how much of my vacation time will be spent waiting for this to happen? While I'm meditating on these considerations, my horse decides to stop for a bite of grass. I'm last in line, and in a half minute the trail of horses ahead of me disappears into a thick grove of trees. Then the saddle slips, and I'm pretty certain I'm going to fall, but before I do, I try to extricate myself. Then I'm on the ground, looking up at the horse, at the sky, calculating the distance I have fallen, wondering which of my bones is broken and how to explain it to my climbing partner.

I have landed on my side, and my hip is the likely candidate, but it's not broken. So I'm fine. Except that I feel like I've been in a car wreck. Bruises will bloom on my hip and side, causing me to wonder, if I weren't so fat, would I still have bruised there? Or would I have just shattered my rib cage?

I walk the horse back to the group. I can't see how this was my fault, and I do my best to keep from being treated like an idiot. I do not enjoy the rest of the ride, thinking on a couple occasions that the horse has tried to bite my toes and then pretend that he didn't. Plus the keys are locked in the car.

The stable owner feels badly that I've fallen, so quickly fetches me a coat hanger and offers the use of a phone.

The coat hanger is not going to work. Then some nice young thugs from the Detroit suburbs offer me this idea: the antenna can be taken off and forced through the rubber molding with far more authority than a coat hanger. In about ten minutes this is accomplished, and I drive off: the car is not ruined, the afternoon not wasted, my hip not broken. Life is good. About an hour later, I remember that my hat was under the car.

This was a hat with a serious brim, a hat meant to thwart skin cancer, a hat I bought in Bridgeport, California, after sitting behind a guy in church whose ears had been roasted and swollen to the size of sausages. It was a cool hat, and I've never seen one like it before or since. It is gone. Okay. Fine. I've got two days of vacation left. Chill. That's what you do on vacation. Run for an hour each day. Drive carefully. Live carefully on the horizontal plane, so that I'll be fully prepared to die on the vertical.

The vacation ends nicely. In fact, with the exception of the glasses, the horse, and the hat, it's all been nice. Once home I have twenty-four hours to pack for Chamonix. It won't be hard—I've been making lists all summer. I check on my Oakleys. I didn't want to take them on vacation and lose them on the beach—they are too cool. But the Oakleys aren't there. Where I left them. In my top dresser drawer. In their silk pouch. The first thing you see when you open the drawer.

There were various workers in our home over the two weeks we were absent, and this is the only possible explanation I can consider for the disappearance of my Oakleys. And yet I trust two of the workers unquestioningly. This situation depresses me far out of proportion to its seriousness, perhaps because the glasses were an extravagance to begin with. My wife suggests that I hid them to thwart just such a possibility, or that I am suffering from absent-mindedness: witness my reading glasses and my hat. I argue that I know precisely where I last saw those items. I am planning to take ginkgo biloba to counteract the possible effects of altitude, noting that it is also recommended for Alzheimer's patients.

As I pack, the missing sunglasses continue to vex me. The sunglasses, the hat, the horse, the locked keys, the reading glasses—all are seemingly connected to my lack of preparation for this climbing, not to mention the ghost of Dave Kahn. I'm not a relaxed traveler or a sound sleeper. I have a twenty-four-hour journey ahead of me, with numerous plane changes. A loss of luggage will mean the trip is basically doomed. Also, the weather—if that is bad, there is no alternative plan. All these worries find their focus in my missing sunglasses, the ones I probably shouldn't have bought anyway.

As I drive to the airport, I am still obsessing about the glasses. I find it literally depressing. And the fact that I am so bothered by it bothers me more than the missing glasses themselves. At O'Hare I pass shop after shop, opportunity after opportunity, to replace them with precisely the same pair. On the plane I take out a book: *Robinson Crusoe*, which I have selected to teach in the fall—a scant two weeks away—despite not having read it in a dozen years. Crusoe, it turns out in the early pages, "had several times loud Calls from my Reason and my more composed Judgment to go home, yet I had no Power to do it." Despite the "plain and visible Token" that he should not become a seafaring man, Crusoe is compelled to do otherwise. The thought wears me out. I toss back my Scotch and Benadryl (not a recommendation) and doze off and on while the worst movie ever made flashes soundlessly above me, and the Atlantic does likewise below.

When I reach Geneva and my baggage arrives, when John is there precisely as planned and the car rented, when I tell him the whole pathetic story—which he politely ignores—as we pay the toll and speed toward Chamonix, I am beginning to think that the glass was, as John so clearly thinks and as I usually think, *half full.* The weather looks good.

By the time we get to the *télécabine* at Les Houches, it's early afternoon. By the time John has packed his stuff in the *télécabine* parking lot, midafternoon. By the time we take the lift to the train station, we've missed the train and have an hour-plus wait. The 4:30 train.

Thus it is that we begin hiking at near five o'clock. Not what you call an alpine start, nor even a crack-of-noon start. I'd set out at a later hour before, but I don't want to think now about how those excursions turned out. The weather is threatening to bother the hell out of us, and so we begin.

After an hour we're in our rainsuits, we're in whiteout, we're drenched. Lightning is striking around us, and it's cold. Alpine.

We have no idea where the hut is.

Then the hail begins. Finally, we realize that most likely we have overshot the hut, but it appears below us across a snowfield just before the sun sets irrevocably. We trudge over to it.

We remind the skeptical hut keeper that we have made reservations at the wrong hut but that we've been promised a space on the floor of the Goûter Hut. We walk into a hut occupied by seventy European men, average age about sixty years, who eye us with suspicion. Why is everyone so old? I wonder. The youngsters are all out parapenting and taking Ecstasy?

We're just making it more crowded for them, plus we obviously don't know what we're doing, arriving in damned near darkness, all soaked and fucked up. I remove my bright yellow Lance Armstrong "Two-Time Tour de France Winner" hat, and we nudge a space for ourselves at a table. The hut keeper brings us hot soup and bread and a beer, and it all begins to feel very civilized despite the wet-dog smell emanating from . . . us. Yes, very civilized, until it's time to sleep, which will clearly be impossible. We're on foam pads under one of the dining tables. I have slept under a table before, but the circumstances were murkier. We're resting, I tell myself: rest is good.

The masses are moving. I look at my watch, as I have been doing every four minutes or so since first lowering myself under the table. It's about 12:30 A.M. A tired-looking fellow apologizes for the noise, complaining bitterly about the insanity of these early starts. The rule, unenforced here, is that people are supposed to sleep until the somewhat more civilized hour of two o'clock. The tired-looking fellow is bellowing his complaint in English, as it seems that we are the only people who understand him.

He is a guide, it turns out. His clients appear after a while, speechless and near comatose. Meanwhile, the guide, whose name we learn later to be Smiler, gives us a stern lecture on the dangers of the Grand Couloir, the need to cross it early, the fact that a dozen people a year die there. A dozen people a year? In one spot in the Alps? How inglorious, how anonymous! No *Into Thin Air* for these folks—mere sacrificial pilgrims on the holy mountain.

We are concerned, to say the least. However, since sleep is not really an option, it's not as if there's any possibility of losing sleep over it. Our current plan is to rest for a few more hours and then light out ahead of a second wave of climbers aiming for the Goûter Hut, a mere thousand meters above us. This first wave is heading all the way to the summit from here; we're merely going to the Goûter. Smiler's party will go all the way up to the summit and back down to the Goûter tonight. We're going slower on the ascent; later we'll be faced with the question of a long descent, or another night on the hut floor.

After the first wave of climbers leaves, we abandon our spaces beneath the community dining tables and jump up into bunks, where it is gloriously quiet and warm. We sleep for three hours and wake amazed by the fact.

We are able to get a fast start and thus find ourselves at the dreaded couloir in an ideal position—with no one above us kicking down stones and still early enough that no melting has occurred. The crossing goes smoothly: we zip across singly and unroped, while the other keeps eyes and ears fixed above for signs and sounds of rockfall.

This is a ridge climb up to the hut. A west ridge, thus we are in shadow in the morning. The trail has been filled in with last night's hailstorm, so we're basically on snow. It's just fine most of the way up. We reach a large crucifix marking the death of a climber—by lightning, I'm guessing, based on the previous evening's experience and the exposed location on the ridge. "Forgive us our sins," I translate from the Latin. The date of the demise is August 14, 1953.

"Hey," I say to John, "check out the date. That's today."

"You really are superstitious, aren't you?"

Not to mention the year—the year we were born.

"Yeah," I say, "I really am."

When the sun breaks over the mountains, John pulls out *his* new sunglasses: prescription Julbos, iridium blue lenses. An extravagance, John says, an indulgence. I am wearing some junky glasses possessing a notion of cool to which I no longer subscribe. Yet I like the idea of not having spent money on sunglasses—then remember not only that I did spend the money on them, but I don't even have the glasses.

The route continues nicely until we run into the long train of descending climbers. Among them is a trio of Brits who relate to us the tale of their previous evening, when they were struck by lightning. Numerous times.

"So I says, 'Wot's that smell?' And then I realize it's me hair!"

One lad was "choppered off," struck insensible. The others are retreating merely stunned, with the aid of Nigel, another philanthropic Brit.

"We'd be lost without Nigel."

They were giddy with the idea of being alive, still new to them. "Well, you've got a hell of a story to tell," I rationalize.

"I'd have rather tagged the summit, mate."

"Lots of people can tell that story," I offer in consolation.

Soon we are at the hut, where we have a large bowl of pasta with Bolognese sauce and take a midafternoon nap. When we emerge, Smiler is there among the masses, his clients having disappeared somewhere to lick their wounds. We spend the afternoon talking climbing. Friends in common, places in common. Common in a rarefied sort of way. I file away in my mind that he's done five of the six great north faces in the Alps, the only one left undone being the only one possibly within the range of my feeble abilities, the North Face of the Piz Badile.

After dinner we retire en masse to the bunks, where I doze off for perhaps as long as an hour of uninterrupted sleep. We awaken, also en masse, and are on our way by 2:45 A.M.—in about the middle of the train. It is cold, as we've been advised it would be. It's frustrating for a while to be caught in this great line, but soon we begin passing whole ropes of people, others fall off the pace, and we are under the illusion that we are on our own—which, in truth, we are. Of what help could anyone up there be to us? Indeed, of what help might I be to them? We're moving upward a step at time; the energy required for any act of altruism would be hard to muster. The main thing about the climb is that it's very long: section after section rears up above us. We find ourselves saying repeatedly, "That can't be as bad as it looks," and that turns out to always be true.

The sun begins rising to our left, lighting up the faces of the Aiguilles, Mont Blanc du Tacul, and Mont Maudit, which are beginning to drop away below us. The moon, full but no longer above us, is setting in the west. We are ascending a ridge that rises between the sun and the moon, bathed in one or the other's surreal light. Before the sun rises into view it casts the shadow of the mountain to the west, a perfect triangle floating just below the horizon. And we're going up, and up. Breath, one, two, three, breath. A couple Grateful Dead lines appear in my head, unbidden, cycling through in mindless loops:

> Everything movin' here but much too slowly
> Little bit quicker and we might have time
> to say "how do you do?" before we're left behind.

The summit will never come, will never come, and then it appears suddenly—a flattening of the ridge, the highest point in all of Europe: France, Italy, and Switzerland at our feet.

John's camera is frozen. We spend maybe ten minutes up there. It's taken us three and a half hours from the hut—excellent time (three to five is typical), and we're descending. We slow to a crawl and it's déjà vu all over again, John having this weird habit of melting down after a successful ascent. My feeling is that we should push all the way down so we can catch the last train at about 5:00 P.M. Considering we have no lodging arranged at either of the huts, this seems more sensible than another sleepless night under the table. There is the problem of the rockfall in the couloir, worsened by midday sun— and of course the problem of descending nine thousand feet in a single push.

Getting back to the hut takes us nearly as long as our ascent. Here John faces the reality of our need to descend all the way to Chamonix. This fact, coupled with the fear of crossing the couloir, about which we have been incessantly warned, makes relaxing difficult despite being inside the hut. A half pint of beer and a long nap would be ideal. Crossing the couloir in the early morning before the sun warms the rocks and sends them careening down would also be ideal. In climbing, the ideal usually outpaces its seekers.

We slurp our soup, our toes freed from mountain boots, assess our windburn and energy levels. Outside, the clouds roll by with a speed that appears induced by time-lapse photography, with plenty of blue sky between them. I have a photograph somewhere of John taken near the end of our descent of the Monte Rosa twenty years earlier. It's not possible to discern whether he is alive, a ring of vomit burned into the snow. That was a long day. Typically, tagging a summit in the Alps means a long day, mostly because it starts so early. John is not enthusiastic about going down to Chamonix, but we feel there is no choice. Feeling that you have no choice in the mountains is not necessarily a good feeling, but it beats indecision.

We plod downward, past the spot where we had met the lightning-struck Brits, to the bottom of the ridge where the couloir must be crossed. Here a number of people are grouped, bottlenecked to gather the courage to sprint across the shooting gallery. They are clumped together in a sketchy silence, like boys deciding who will be first to jump off the bridge into the water. The couloir itself looks like a runway down which large rocks tumble sporadically in huge, slow-motioned leaps of space. So far as we can see, there are never two rocks falling at once, and though they tumble silently, they usually announce their approach. It looks manageable. The actual danger zone may be only forty feet across, though it's probably better measured by the number of seconds (seconds? well, less than two minutes) it will take to cross. But if it's not really dangerous, then why do so many people die here? They are, slow, beat, inexperienced, we rationalize. Unlucky.

I watch a large flat rock spin downward, a stone thrown to skip on water, which isn't far off. It builds speed as it descends, but it's hard to believe you couldn't dodge it, even in crampons on the slope. The rock approaches like a loping roundhouse of a hook that the boxer sees coming for what feels like interminable seconds yet somehow has been powerless to avoid, smashing into his temple; he's surprised, as if he hadn't seen it coming at all. But he had.

Nevertheless, we sprinted across, and shortly after, we began the hike out to the train station, the problem being that if we didn't catch the five o'clock train we would have to spend another night out, this time without sleeping bags, because the walk to Les Houches would be unthinkable after the length of our day, which was approaching fifteen hours.

John and I have fallen into a pattern on our descents in which our paces grow farther apart as the day lengthens. Thus when I arrive at the train station a couple hours later, I can't guess how long it will be until John arrives. So long as we make the train, it's all good. We make our train, and not too long after that we're seated at a sidewalk table at the Cafe de L'M, where the placemats match the view of the Aiguilles—the needles—and as our exhaustion sets in, the alpenglow brightens and fades, leaving the ridge to the Goûter hut, the Dome de Goûter, and the distant summit silhouetted against the night sky.

We spend a rest day playing tourist (playing? No, we *are* tourists). I imagine Dave Kahn walking the streets of Chamonix during the days before his death on the Dru. The cemetery is filled with just such people. We do not go to the cemetery, nor do we take the train up to Argentière to look up in wonderment at the Dru, coincidentally (or not) the mountain on which Royal Robbins and Gary Hemming made the most significant American first ascent in the Alps, the American Direct in 1963. Kahn, dead now for over twenty years, was drawn here by the same desires that draw me still. Defoe's Crusoe: "I know not what to call this, nor will I urge, that it is a secret overruling Decree that hurries us on to be the Instruments of our own Destruction, even tho' it be before us, and that we rush upon it with our Eyes open."

The next day is a rain-soaked effort in the Aiguilles Rouges, where we make it to the base of La Chapelle de la Glière before the deluge.

Finally, on the day before the trip ends, we find ourselves on the *téléphérique* at the base of the Aiguille du Midi. The weather is iffy once again—cloudy with occasional spitting rain. It is not expected to get worse. Or better. *C'est la vie.*

We are setting out to climb the Arête des Cosmiques, the famous south ridge of the Aiguille du Midi. To do this climb one rides the *téléphérique* to the summit of the Aiguille du Midi, where there is a restaurant and observation decks. You walk through a tunnel near the top of the mountain that lets you off on the summit of the northeast ridge, which you descend to the glacier below, the Vallée Blanche, a route whose ascent the great French alpinist Gaston Rébuffat describes as "banal and laborious." Depending on the snow conditions—and the number of travelers, the season, and the time of day—this can be an easy walk down a staircase of snow or a death climb. The first time I did it twenty years earlier, it seemed like a death climb. This time it is easy, but quite probably the conditions are the same now as then and it is I, with twenty years of mountain travel behind me, who have changed.

Though the descent to the Vallée Blanche does not take long, perhaps twenty minutes, this is enough time for the mountain to appear to rise up suddenly in a looming mass. Now we traverse under the imposing south face to the west, past the Éperon des Cosmiques, and gain the south ridge—the Arête des Cosmiques—near its beginning.

The ridge is named not for its cosmic qualities—of which there happen to be many: gendarmes and towers, couloirs of ice and snow—but for the fact that near its base is a cosmic-ray laboratory. Why there, and what exactly a cosmic-ray laboratory is, are questions that are beyond me. I tend to forget about the etymology of the name and think of the climb as a short walk in the alpine cosmos. Lines from the Grateful Dead's "Cosmic Charley" run through my head while I shift my attention alternately to the ice and rock under my feet, the route beyond, and the ever-threatening sky above us.

> I just wonder if you shouldn't feel
> less concern about the great unreal.

Typical Robert Hunter lyrics: you sense deep meaning but can't articulate in your own words what it might be. Here I am climbing through the great unreal, but I can't see becoming less concerned.

The route is short, and John has done it before: these factors alleviate somewhat my concerns about the weather. When we find the crux, a tough moment of aid climbing, I am relieved to know that we are on route but suddenly distressed to realize how difficult the move is. The move is *obligatoire*—which I have seen translated into English as "compulsory." But I prefer *obligatoire*—one is *obligated* to do the move, it is your obligation—which sounds to me like the language of religion: a holy day of obligation. Climbing is a spiritual obligation.

The move is puzzling and awkward, but nonetheless it takes only minutes, and once I manage to raise the front point of my crampon into the god-knows-how-old hanging nylon etrier, I can't really tell you how it was accomplished. Our walk through the alpine cosmos continues, winding our way among the gendarmes until the summit platform is in sight.

Rébuffat has said that "you should avoid looking up too often towards the summit, that is, the concrete platform built for the tourist and the television mast, both unrelievedly ugly."

The ridgeline has flattened out, and we can see, just ahead, a ladder that reaches up to the observation platform. How many times had I wished for one on the summit of mountains: a ladder appearing like a deus ex machina to take one to safety.

As we sit to take off our crampons, coil the rope, and let our guard down, we are conscious that the very tourists of whom Rébuffat despairs have been videotaping the last meters of our ascent. We have appeared out of the mists from a cold and unseen world below for their especial pleasure. I am pleased that we have finished the climb before the weather deteriorates, pleased to have sneaked another climb in at all. Typically a summit is not particularly relaxing: most accidents happen during the descent, late in the day when one is exhausted. But here we have the sense of being down already when we have just arrived at the top—it's early in the day, we are not exhausted. Soon we will be whisked down to Chamonix in the comfort of a *téléphérique* cabin. Artificial, yes, but pleasing. We are conscious, yes, of being observed, and it's a bit awkward, this being on of the easier climbs in the range. Just then a voice bellows out from above:

"Is that John McInerney and David Stevenson?"

What the hell? We are in France. Near the summit of a mountain. Who is talking? God? And why is he speaking English?

But no, it's Jim Balog, a climbing friend of John's from their undergraduate days together (twenty-four years earlier) and acquaintance of mine also. Balog is a professional photographer, but he's not working now—he's showing his daughter Europe, the grand tour.

We ascend the ladder and straddle the railing to marvel at the cosmic coincidence of our meeting. Climbing is, in essence, a private act. To be witnessed actually finishing a climb is an odd feeling, simultaneously a kind of violation and validation. Jim seemed unsurprised—but of course, here you are, climbers climbing. What else would you be doing? As if it were the most natural thing in the world.

We have Jim take our photos on the platform with our point-and-shoots, joking that we now own exclusive prints by "James Balog, photographer." We await the downward *téléphérique* with a sense of leisurely catching up, talking effusively, trying to include his daughter in our after-the-climb banter. We are on the streets of Chamonix before we know it, arranging to meet later for dinner. And now the climbing trip is over.

For days I have not thought of my missing sunglasses and hat. Nor have I thought about being thrown from the horse. ("You mean you fell off the horse," a horse-person friend says.) The crucifixes and memorials that dot the trails and routes of the alpine ridges, the cemeteries, Dave Kahn: I do not think of these now. I have long since given up trying to extract meaning from my mountain excursions. Meeting Balog at the top of the Aiguille du Midi: chance. The odds are long, of course, but to attach any meaning to it says more about the process of making meaning than it does about what is actually there.

I cut myself a modicum of slack: I'm a tad less of a poser.

I am on the plane flying westward, nearing my home in the midwestern United States. There out the window is Lake Michigan, its white beaches curving northward toward the beach at Ludington. The angle of the plane and the contour of the beach coalesce into a large question mark. What, I wonder, is the lake trying to ask me?

2000

STRUCK

Longs Peak, Rocky Mountains

Today, many so-called proponents of alpine climbing
are actually engaged in "Guaranteed Outcome Climbing." Guaranteed Outcome Climbing is ... regressive.
—Scott Backes in American Alpine Journal, 2001

OVERDUE, WEATHER, EXHAUSTION, EXCEEDING ABILITIES
McBroom and Ford were the third party within two
weeks to have endured an unplanned bivouac on
Kiener's Route, resulting in a forty-hour climb and
descent of the peak. Similar incidents have also com-
monly occurred here at this time of the season in other
years, resulting in cold injuries and even death.
—Accidents in North American Mountaineering, 2001

The drive. 100 degrees, no air-conditioning. Wind pouring through
the windows. The stereo semiaudible, stuck on one station.

Looming over the freeway just east of Kearney, Nebraska, is the
Great Platte River Road Archway Monument, an architectural mon-
strosity that spans the freeway and has risen out of the prairie since
my last drive west, two years earlier. It appears to connect nothing to
nothing. I don't stop, but the literature describes it as a place where
travelers can contemplate the westward migration on the nation's
busiest transcontinental highway; to this is added the qualifier "in
the context of the pioneers." "Infrared headsets," we are told, "relate
first-person stories of early travelers." A neat trick, no doubt, even
for the infrared technology.

I'm not sure of the exact source of my cynicism. Maybe it's that for
me the West is associated with nature, the wilder the better. Despite
my misgivings, I think about the rhetorical questions asked by the

museum display concerning those pioneers: "What happened to them? What places did they find? Were they rewarded?"

We find, in essence the same questions at the end of Thoreau's "Ktaddn," or printed on the bottom of Gauguin's largest South Seas painting: "Where do we come from? What are we? Where are we going?" Perhaps also in the minds of Carmelite postulants, seekers.

Tacos in Kearney. Two white kids serving up the grease. One kid has the shirt that says "Rulz? We don't want no steen-king rulz around here."

The air cools off at night, and I feel extra guilt for getting a forty-dollar hotel room instead of a fifteen-dollar campsite. Soft.

A town in Kansas announces itself as Gateway to the West. Highway 36, the sign says, is the straightest line between Indianapolis and Denver. I think of Charlie's question, after the long drive from Macomb, Illinois, to California: "Did you see any wildlife?"

Through eastern Colorado I'm thinking of the unadorned prose of Kent Haruf's *Plainsong*. Maybe prose style really is landscape-driven—a point I often argue against. I arrive in Denver sooner than I had thought possible, stunned by the smog and traffic. I go straight through to Boulder and Neptune, high on my list of favorite climbing shops, where I feel old and out of it. Then up to the Flatirons for a walk below the crags.

I am in the mountains.

I crossed the Mississippi in my first hour from home, and I've driven through or under a number of "gateways" and crossed the plains. But if the terrain doesn't take on some vertical relief—mountains—it doesn't feel like the West to me. Of course, by that measure I've been "west" in New Hampshire and West Virginia, even though my compass would have read east or south as I traveled there.

In his memoir *Lighting Out*, Dan Duane describes climbing as "some kind of near mystical dance, way out west, way up on walls." He's writing about Yosemite Valley, a place that is geographically east of the scene of his writing, east of where he was raised. The quality of westness to which he aspires is clearly a state of mind—Yosemite is simply the best place for it to occur.

Now, below the Flatirons, it rains lightly, even though the sun is out; each drop of liquid catching its light. The uphill is killing me. All around are people who are on vacation, as well as locals for whom a run in the foothills is a daily ritual. I see a muscle-bound mountain athlete of my own age and note that I relinquished membership in that club long ago. I'm an overweight tourist from the Midwest with no chance whatever at succeeding on Longs Peak the next day. After I've checked into the hotel, there is a two-hour downpour and lightning storm. The weather has been unsettled all summer. My friend John's plane arrives late. It's 2 A.M. and a third of a bottle of Talisker before we get to sleep.

The backcountry permit, which I have reserved weeks in advance, asks our helmet and rope colors. This way our bodies can be more readily identified when they are found battered and lifeless at the foot of the difficulties.

In the trailhead parking lot next to my car is another car with Illinois plates. When I say I'm from Macomb, he says, "Macomb, that's … primitive, isn't it?" It's raining too hard to sort gear and pack up, but the clouds blow over in an hour. Our crack-of-noon start has devolved to 5:00 P.M. I think back to other climbs begun at this hour—not a confidence-inspiring list. We stagger into the bivy site at Chasm Lake in near pitch darkness. But we've made good time even if we're beat.

We are sharing the bivouac site with two hot young climbers readying for a tough route on the Diamond, the huge east face of Longs Peak. One kid has recently been up Lamb's Slide, the thousand-foot snow couloir that is the central feature of our route. He tells us it's hard glare ice. He thinks we're doomed without ice screws and gives us complicated alternatives that we're too tired to concentrate on. At some point I realize his experience, however hot on rock, might be limited on glaciers, and conditions might not be so bad as he describes. "Where are you from?" he asks. I hate that question mostly because I hear it as "Where do you live now?" "Illinois where?" he asks. West central, but where exactly? I usually don't say where exactly because it's not a place anyone has ever heard of. "Macomb," I say, because he has insisted. "No way," he says. "I was born in Macomb."

It is the night of the Perseid meteor shower. Shooting stars streak across the sky from horizon to horizon, so bright and long-lasting that each of us sees all of them. No one wants to close their eyes to this show.

In the morning I realize I have slept as soundly and comfortably as I ever slept in the wild. I feel great. Weirdly enough, John feels the same. We expect the ice field, Lamb's Slide, to be impassable. But it is not.

We climb up on the left side of the ice. I'm putting a piece of protection in the rock at the edge of the ice every sixty feet or so. Theoretically these would hold us if I fall. This is not nearly often enough for John, who tends to leave the ice for the highly debatable safety of the rock when possible. Finally we reach the point at which we must cross the ice field and enter Broadway, the fifteen-foot-wide ledge that bisects the east face horizontally for a thousand feet. Crossing the ice field without ice screws means that if either of us falls, we fall to the end of the rope. It is unclear whether the rope will reach across. If it does not, John has extracted a promise from me that I will return to the left side rather than make him simul-climb with me for a few feet until I can reach the safety of the other side.

I make it just barely—the rope is stretching—and he follows with no problem. Broadway is, as advertised, wide and grassy. Shortly we cross the big chimney and find ourselves at the start of the technical difficulties. Two or three pitches of lower fifth-class climbing. Then a jumble of class 3 and 4—scrambling—upward and to the right. Just before the top, we get boxed in by vertical and overhanging rock, and I lead a pitch harder than we had expected. A couple exiting the Casual Route—a route that is far from casual—tell us we are off route, which we have by now figured. Moments later, we're on the summit. The rain has held off, but one never feels relaxed with so many miles to go.

This not being relaxed leads us to decide to return down the standard Keyhole Route—essentially a walk-off—rather than down the north face, which we have seen from across the mountain. The north face would involve multiple rappels from a single rope and then a lot of guessing—"following your nose," as the kid from Macomb said. The walk-off would be much longer. We run the plan past a guy on top. I understand, he says, no stress. Exactly. Just follow the fried eggs, the guy says. I nod, having no idea whatsoever what the fried eggs are. It's a walk-off; we'll find it.

Our chosen route of ascent, Kiener's, was the first route accomplished on the east side of the mountain and was done in winter in 1925. Walter Kiener and Agnes Vaille completed the ascent but not the descent. Vaille died of exposure after hours of below-zero temperatures, and Kiener lost his toes and fingertips to frostbite. Now we're descending the regular route, just as Kiener and Vaille did.

The fried eggs turn out to be red circles with yellow interiors painted on the rocks. They're easy to follow, but the route is long and disorienting. The mountain is huge, and not having ascended this way, we recognize none of the landmarks. Plus, because our descent route has changed, I'm going to have to race into the bivy site at Chasm Lake, where we left our overnight gear, and meet John at the junction with the main trail with our sleeping pads and bags. I'm descending faster than John, a familiar scenario in our long partnership. Instead of having me descend ahead and pick up the stuff, we decide to stay together.

Nonetheless I get further and further ahead. Finally I reach the Keyhole and I get down to the Boulderfield, the site of Agnes Vaille's death. Apparently lots of features on this route are named, but we don't know the names. I wait at the Boulderfield for half an hour until John comes into view at the Keyhole. I figure it might take him another hour to reach the Boulderfield, so I leave instructions with people to tell him to meet me at the junction to Chasm Lake. I figure I can get the bivy stuff and be back at the junction by the time he gets there, or close to it.

As I descend I feel pretty good, moving fast. I've been powering down caffeine all day long. I ask some more people on the trail to tell John to meet me at the junction.

Once I reach the junction, I ditch the rope and hardware under a rock as the weather begins shifting definitively for the worse. As I get close to Chasm Lake, the sky has blackened menacingly. Thunder claps and lightning strikes. It is hailing. I have no parka, and I am beginning to become acutely aware of my lack of water intake. I hike on, the hail pounding me. Before I get soaked to the skin, I duck under an overhang, popping hailstones into my mouth. Lightning is the only real danger; I am idiotically confident the hail will let up. And it does, after about twenty minutes or half an hour.

The hail has yielded an unexpected bonus: it has filled in the trail, making it stand out like a number in a test for color-blindness. I easily pick my way through the scree slope to the bivy spot. There I find the two lads from the night before. They finished their climb, descended the route we decided against, and are waiting out the storm in the bivy cave. They have water, but not much. I now have the water filter, but no water bottles. I drink the liquid out of a can of mandarin oranges and share the oranges with the lads, recalling that John and I had a single can of mandarin oranges up in the Cascades on Mount Stuart in 1975, benighted a couple hundred feet below the summit without water. These oranges are just as good as those. One kid says, "I thought I hated these things, but they taste great!" He'll hate them again soon enough.

I walk out to the junction and collect all the stuff I had left behind, now hail-soaked and weighty.

I can't see any sign of John, and I can see a long way. I walk up the trail for half an hour. No sign of him. I walk back to the junction: how long to wait? It's eight o'clock. I decide to go down, thinking he must have consciously decided to stay up there—even at the slowest possible pace, he would be here by now. Or else he didn't get the messages, found a second wind, and is already at the car. Neither is plausible, but I can think of no other alternatives.

It's one foot in front of the other, and soon darkness is upon me. The trail—supposedly the superhighway of trails—becomes littered with rocks and roots. I find I can't do simple math problems: if it's 6 miles from Boulderfield to the ranger station and the junction is 3.5 miles from the ranger station, how many miles have I gone, and how many to go? This simple calculation is befuddling.

My body is steaming as the air cools. I'm like a cow just out of the heated barn on a midwinter day. My breath is creating a cloud of condensation in front of me, and the light from my headlamp is caught in the cloud. I see a Perrier bottle sitting on the side of the trail near the Goblin Forest. But as I get closer, I see it is a green plant growing by the side of the rail, its petals holding moisture that glints in my headlight like green glass.

The whole time, I'm figuring that John is somewhere above, and in the morning I will have to jog up with water and help him down. He twisted his ankle or simply ran out of gas. Or he's at the car.

But he's not at the car when I get there at 9:45. I lay out my sleeping bag but can't sleep. Too tired, too much caffeine, worrying about John, whatever. I hear cars arrive and parties beginning their ascent. They talk in loud voices, thinking themselves alone: "That will be so fucking cool when we wake up and there's this big fucking mountain right in front of us!"

John shows up at midnight, pissed. We sort it out: wrong junction. None of our reasoning, of course will hold up to examination by well-rested, fully hydrated human beings, so we don't dwell much on it.

By the time Frederick Chapin published *Mountaineering in Colorado* in 1889, he had already observed: "Fortunate will be the adventurer who finds anything of note that has not already been seen and written about by indefatigable members of search parties that have preceded him."

I suppose he was right, except why then do I find this world so fresh and full of possibility every time I venture out and up into it?

Now we drive down to our campsite. On the road is a gigantic elk, breath steaming in the night air, so large it looks as if it could easily leap over the car. I remember driving out from Mount Stuart all those years ago. We were young, and the extra night out hadn't touched us. We had put beer in the stream to cool. As we drove down an old Forest Service road, a moose appeared out of nowhere and blocked the entire road, regarding us coolly and unrushed.

That was twenty-six years earlier, and now, although I can't say that the years have not taken their toll on us, I do know that the mountains and their many gifts have lost none of their power to strike us with awe and wonder.

2003

IN THE BUGS

In the Canadian Rockies

In Banff we first search, as always, for gifts for the family. John can find no T-shirts with the word *Bugaboos*. He confesses to me that he owns 150 T-shirts. This should come as no surprise, as I was probably with him when he bought half of them. Further, there are no postcards of the Bugaboos available in Banff. We wonder what this means, having noticed earlier that Bugaboo Glacier Provincial Park exists on no maps.

We manage to find the road to the Bugs—thirty miles on gravel with tiny signs marking the forks in the road. John, whom I might describe as typically prudent, is driving the living crap out of the rental car, a Chrysler Sebring, about twice as fast as I would be going. A bit out of character, but maybe not, when you consider his affinity for Meat Loaf's *Bat out of Hell*. John must be psyched! The parking lot full to capacity. We rig chicken wire, rocks, and sticks to protect the vehicles against the porcupines who eat the hoses and tires.

The packs are killing us. Sixty pounds? Two young sprinters pass us on the trail. Then three more. We hit the hut at the three-hour mark and hike another hour, up eight hundred more feet to Applebee Meadows. We are ascending an eastward-draining watercourse, traveling west and then up a south face in fading daylight—the same as the approach to Iceberg Lake at the base of Whitney's east face, the same as up to the lower saddle below the Grand Teton. It's about dark when we arrive, and we are basically too hammered to eat. I am wondering about how many of these big-assed backpacking approaches I have left in me.

The next day, I feel sort of okay. The weather is perfect, and I feel we should be climbing. But John insists that a rest day is necessary, and it surely is for him and probably is for me as well. Of course, if the weather turns bad later, I'll regret the rest day mightily. I walk around, scout the path to the glacier. We move our tent and lie about. I have no inclination to read, probably because the only book I have brought is *Gravity's Rainbow*. The day just kind of drifts by. Stoney and Joe, the two trail sprinters, show up at 10 A.M., having been up to the summit of Bug Spire via the northeast ridge and back via the Kain in an amazing six hours. Other people we talked to took eighteen hours, and it's said that you can see headlights bobbing around near the summit long after dark, evidence of the benighted.

The next day we do the Kain Route of Bugaboo. It's long. How many roped pitches? Five of low-fifth-class simul-climbing, then one real hard one, then two more roped pitches. This is stacked on top of about a thousand vertical feet of class 3 stuff. When we get to the beginning of the fifth-class climbing, there are two guys on a ledge. One is clinging to the ledge with his back to the rock; the other is bleeding heavily from his head. The bleeder, it turns out, is the leader, his frightened friend a first-timer. The bleeder wants us to take him up with us, leaving his friend on the ledge. He says he moves pretty fast, considering, and he lifts up his pant leg to reveal a plastic and steel leg.

We suggest he'd best not leave his friend there on the ledge. He understands.

The crux is at the Gendarme, first climbed by Conrad Kain in 1916. When Canadians speak of him, they do so as if he were a personal friend, as if he might show up around the next bend in the trail, even though he's been dead since 1934 (at fifty-one—one year older than I). The 5.6 rating is the crux, though according to a guide we meet as he's descending, "the only problem is that it's not 5.6." No one wants to admit that Kain led 5.8 in 1916, so they call it a 6. Great.

Turns out it's a little harder than a 6, but probably not an 8. And really it's just one move that's real hard, and it's well protected. It goes quickly. We're on the summit a couple pitches later and then, as ever, quickly on our way down. At the rappel anchors we meet three young guys ascending. This lets us actually enjoy the summit, because we can't leave it until they pass. We had actually passed these guys earlier—they had been a tad off route. So as we're waiting for them to get out of the way, John, who is feeling loquacious, offers them this unsolicited advice, his Sermon on the Mount: "So, if your wife tells you that she's leaving you because of your climbing, that's not it." I act outraged and tell him not to darken their youthful, optimistic outlook. The descent goes smoothly, except for the fact that we were out of water before we reached the summit, and my rock shoes are eating my toes alive.

The next day is a rest day, but the weather is good, and I do a scramble up Eastpost Spire, which has a very nice summit and a terrific cloud show. I'm with four younger climbers from the Seattle area. On the way down we go for a numbing swim for a few seconds in one of the little glacier lakes. I was totally peer pressured into it, embarrassed by my white briefs, not to mention white belly spilling over the waistband.

The next day John and I do the West Ridge of Pigeon Spire in threatening weather. The party ahead of us turns back a couple pitches up out of fear of lightning. A helicopter thwacks its way up one of the glaciers, unseen by us. The climbing is wonderfully easy—low fifth-class—never hard. The routefinding is pretty obvious, because it's a ridge. It is said that one person a year dies here soloing this route, but that seems like talk. It is also said that this is the best 5.4 in the world—and it gets my vote. Everywhere the route looks hard—really hard—and everywhere it is surprisingly easy. What a pleasure.

We have to run down, and it is raining when we get back to the glacier. By the time we get to the col the rain has stopped, but I am soaked and have put two crampon rips in my pant legs, so maybe I'm more beat than I think I am. I have agreed to rappel down the first part of the col because John doesn't like the bare ice there. I'd rather walk, but in truth the conditions have deteriorated in the days we've been here, and rappelling is clearly the safer choice. We set up the rappel, and I'm off. However, when I reach the end of the rope—that is 165 feet, since we're using a doubled 8-millimeter cord—I find myself not at another fixed anchor but rather in the middle of a horribly steep snowfield fifty yards from any safe haven whatsoever. Fuck me! I rapped off the wrong anchors!! I storm back up in a semi-rage. We set up the new rap, and I'm off again, this time tearing a rip in my thumb so that I'm bleeding into the snow and pissed off. And still, more or less, just standing in the middle of a steep couloir with no anchors. I yell to John to ask if he has any Band-Aids. "No," he yells, "I don't have any mayonnaise." This amuses him so greatly he laughs most of the rest of the way down, over the next two crevasses. I am sour—it's hard to know why exactly (because the trip is over, I suppose, or the climbing, anyway)—and it takes me until we reach a flat spot in the rocks where we decrampon to laugh about the mayonnaise.

We have portioned our Scotch out well and have enough to celebrate our climbs, to toast the Bugaboos, to congratulate ourselves (but not literally, not aloud. After all, we've only just done the two easiest climbs in the range).

The next morning we hear about the woman crushed by a boulder—the helicopter we heard was evacuating her. "You rented a car?" young Dave from the next campsite asks incredulously. "Not that beat-to-shit Sebring?"

Yes, we admitted, that was our car.

Within hours we reach it, the Sebring, hoses and tires apparently uneaten by porcupines. We drive to Lake Louise surrounded on all sides by incredible mountain vistas.

Soon we are drinking the finest single malt Scotch at the Château Lake Louise, looking out at Mount Victoria, a peak we first came here to climb in 1973. We walk along the lake and, speaking for myself here, I feel old. It's been thirty years since I was last there, and I knew then that it was doubtful that I would return. It is near dark, but the peaks to the east are lit up with alpenglow. The trip has been wildly successful and spectacular minute by minute, but now it is over.

2004

The title "Short Walks with McInerney" is a homage to the great Tom Patey essay "A Short Walk with Whillans." John McInerney and I met in junior high school and began going to the mountains together in 1971. Since then there have been very few years that we haven't managed to climb something together. John's editorial influence is such that I defer to his insistence that we drank a third of a bottle of Talisker in Colorado, not half, as I originally wrote.

The three climbs recounted here were done while I lived in rural Illinois, a time when my children were young and my career uncertain. I felt lucky to climb once a year.

In the last lines of the Bugaboo piece, I voice my fear that I will never see Lake Louise again. But circumstances have happily changed, and I have been there often over the last few years, a trend that I expect to continue.

AXE OF
CONTRITION

only the blessed
make
pineneedle tea
—John Mann

"There's a route around there, that starts at about the top of that snowfield. You guys might be able to do it," my friend Woody said. He's local, so he ought to know.

We're standing in a talus field at the base of the Diamond in Wyoming's Snowy Range, looking up at hard, east-facing snow at ten thousand feet in the early morning and dodging snowballs that our kids are lobbing at us from a patch a hundred feet up the slope. They're anxious to get on the rock. I'm just anxious.

The area has no guidebook, a fact I admire in principle, but since I'm with my son Macklin, a thirteen-year-old who's maybe climbed once outside the converted silos of an indoor gym in rural Illinois, I would prefer at least a beer-fueled, pencil-drawn topo on the back of an envelope.

Not to mention that our approach shoes and rock gear leave us underequipped for the snow. Misgivings. If I paid too much attention, nothing would ever get climbed. Woody gives me an ice hammer, the same one we used in the 1970s on a winter climb of Mount Stuart—I have one just like it at home in a milk crate of antique climbing equipment. The angle is not too intimidating, the distance about eighty feet. I hack out steps. A second tool would be nice, I think, wondering how Macklin will deal with this. I reach the rock and slide the hammer down the rope. My anchor making becomes superattenuated when the second is my kid. I'm an asshole; I should always be this careful.

Macklin hasn't belayed me, so there's no anchor for him to break down. He throws on his pack and is hammering his way up the snow as steadily as I can reel in the rope. "We gotta go ice climbing," he says.

The dollars I'd have to spend on ice climbing tools, boots, and crampons for him and his brother spin in my head like the whirling reels in a reservation slot machine. And then I'm already calculating the cost of bailing: descending this snowfield, for example, would be a pain.

Macklin zips up the first fifth-class pitch as smoothly as on the snowfield. The next pitch, the same. Not bad for a gym-trained flat-lander. Plus, he's carrying the water and rain gear, a little food, an alpine pack at altitude.

We're high on the face now: Lake Marie glitters below, and the reddish boulders of the talus field have shrunk to gravelly debris. Occasionally cars can be seen silently winding to or from Snowy Range Pass. Our friends, brother and son, are on the face to the north somewhere, but we can't see or hear them. We have the whole sparkling vertical universe all to ourselves.

"How much more, dad?"

"Hard to say. We're about halfway." I hope that we're a tad farther along than that.

"So, it's easier to keep going, right? It would be hard to go down from here."

"Exactly right."

I pass the water bottle, and he nods in manly acceptance.

As I am climbing the next pitch, dark clouds surge over the face from the west, squeezing all the blue into the distant eastern hori-zon. In near simultaneity the climbing intensifies: where the crack can be protected, it bulges; where the crack thins, it steepens. Hard to climb, hard to protect. Worst of all: at the top of the pitch, blocks the size of ice chests balance delicately one against the other awaiting a butterfly's passing to topple them into the abyss.

Suddenly, I feel panic. God knows why it had taken so long: I have brought my son on this climb where a block could easily drop on his head. In my younger years, my partners and I were cavalier about objective dangers, calling them acts of God, misheard and thereafter known as *axe* of God.

Sure we have helmets. Aluminum foil shields against a nuclear blast. What good would they be?

Macklin requires tension—that I hold the rope tight between us to minimize the length of this fall should he take one. Constant tension. Large raindrops fall in slow motion, splat on my helmet.

He can't extract a wired stopper wedged tightly in a seam of rock. Ten minutes.

"Leave it!" To hell with the nut.

"Tension!"

The blocks. The blocks. I begin to pray, *Oh, my God, I am heartily sorry... for bringing my kid on a climb with loose blocks ... for having offended thee.... All I want is for the rope not to knock the blocks down. Is that too much to ask? I firmly resolve, with the help of Thy grace, to sin no more and to avoid the near occasion of sin. ...* Avoid the near occasion of sin? How the hell do you do that? Stay on the couch?

If something happens to me, Macklin doesn't have the experience to do a damned thing about it. *Contrition.* I hope he would have the sense to anchor himself to the wall and wait for help, but I have neglected to give him any such instruction. Hell yes, I'm *contrite.* This is so much more stupid than soloing, I can't believe it.

Finally, he pulls up and over the edge. "Will we have to rappel?" he asks.

"No," I say, "it's a walk-off." I hadn't even told him that. My God, he trusts me completely. And the prayer? It came to me out of the ether. I hadn't called it to mind in thirty years. Idiot *and* hypocrite. "Once we top out there's a trail. A couple more pitches, maybe."

I remember we didn't bring headlamps. But the blocks have not fallen. The rain is holding off. We even have a couple swigs of water.

I lead up twenty-five feet on solid rock with six-inch ledges between hard moves, easier than anything on the last pitch. From here there's a grassy ramp with a few feet of class 5 that looks like it will top out.

Macklin says he will lead it.

"Go for it." I hand him half a rack, some runners. "Put something in."

But no, it's easy ground, he won't put anything in.

In minutes he's pulled himself over the top and there he stands, arms raised in triumph against the dark clouds roiling overhead.

I scramble to join him. I hold the camera arm's length in front of us, and we put our heads together for a portrait. In the photograph the kid looks composed and serious, a little older than his actual years. His long hair is held off his face by a Japanese bandanna rolled up under his helmet, the master of cool. My helmet looks borrowed, and my expression, if I weren't here to tell you, might belie any number of emotions: happiness, drunkenness, or just relief. The background is darkish, a jumble of lichen-covered boulders leading northward to the true summit. In the mirrored lenses of my sunglasses you can see my arm extended out and pointing the camera back at us. Beyond my arm, nothing but blue sky to the east. Honestly, I look like a fool.

"So when *are* we going ice climbing, Dad?"

During the remaining days of the road trip, we continue climbing. Sporty stuff, no more than a single pitch. I am trying, for a while, to avoid the near occasion of sin.

Amen.

2007

This trip took place in 2006, two years before we left the Midwest for Alaska. The climb remains one of my very favorites, but one that in retrospect, I would not have undertaken, at least not under those circumstances.

The epigraph is from *Wyoming*, poems by John Mann (Finishing Line Press, 2008), inspired by the road trip during which this climb took place.

BYRON GLACIER,
JUNE 24, 2009

My son's first glacier. He, who has been stumbling through his fif-teenth year, moves as if born attached to these ice tools, performing a dance more natural than walking. Even his frontpointing appears effortless, delicate, as if he's tiptoeing up a sidewalk that his heels will never touch, as if youth holds some antidote for ice and gravity. He wants what we all want: more.

Farther, steeper, higher, the whole mountain, and then, of course, another.

He knows I go to the mountains, but I don't think he knows why. And here he is, treating this ice work, this frozen world, with a kind of reverence, as if guessing that for him, too, salvation may be found here.

Now that we cannot pretend they are not shrinking, every visit to a glacier is more sacred than ever. The Byron is so close, our back-yard glacier, an hour by car from Anchorage and only a mile more of flat walking on a well-maintained trail before we enter the primeval world of snow: a jumble of seracs, leaning towers, perfectly named erratics of rock and ice, the alluvial fans of debris where a dozen miniature avalanches have spread their wares as a card dealer fans the deck, *pick a card*.

Random, he says, one of his favorite words. He's right, sure, but I don't like to encourage him: he seems to see the whole world in the word.

A glacier is called alive because it moves, advancing, retreating, a frozen army.

It also speaks. Under the rush of wind, the sound of rushing water. Under the snow, under the ice, creaks and groans, every once in a while a crash, an echo. Ancient, almost translatable, it says "Beware" in every tongue. Jake Breitenbach knew that mountains move. So his famous elegy tells us in Tom Hornbein's *Everest: The West Ridge*, his body entombed in the Khumbu Icefall, 1963. And closer, on Denali, Mugs Stump lies in the crevasse that "swallowed" him "silently, quickly," as his clients said. When I used to see Mugs around town, at the bakery, I was surprised that he walked around, lived, and breathed the same air as the rest of us; if you knew what he'd been doing in the mountains, it would have never occurred to you that he wasn't immortal.

We say, "He died doing what he loved." We say, "He was in the wrong place at the wrong time." We say, "When your number's up, your number's up."

But for us this is the right place and the right time. The mountain won't move.

We will. Upward, we reach the *toe*, or the *head*, opposites that describe that same feature when applied to glaciers: the terminus. Or is this the beginning?

This is the week of the Northern solstice, when time becomes unhinged. "We've got all night, Dad," my son says; he sounds exasperated that I want to stop just after 9 P.M. The sun won't set for hours, but now it's gone behind a ridge. In its shadow, we return to winter. We layer on all our clothes, point out with our axes the possible routes to the summit, etching them into memory for future use.

"Why the ridge and not straight up?" he asks. Damn, I think, day 1 and already with the straight up. I explain the likely paths of the seracs above the *direttissima*, the probable crevasses, and then, for balance, the lesser dangers of the cornices on the ridge. "That's a real word?" he asks. "*Direttissima?*" He looks at me as if for once in his whole life I have told him something possibly useful for navigating the world.

On the way down a new landscape appears: ice chunks, aglow in the twi-night sun, float across Portage Lake like burning ships. Above the lake, more snow and peaks float on the shadowed forest, alight the long alpenglow, gateway to the infinite: Begich, Boggs, Maynard, their names map-learned, not yet experienced.

I think of the way my British friends say the word *glacier*: *glahss-y-ear*, making it sound the enchanted place that it truly is. My son and I have been to the *glahss-y-ear*, but my language won't hold it. "Earth's the right place for love," Frost best said, and like him, I don't know where it's likely to go better.

2009

I began writing this essay very shortly after the experience, a rarity for me. One of my recollections is that while I was thinking about this piece, the great rock climber John Bachar fell to his death soloing near his home in Mammoth Lakes, California, on the east side of the Sierra. Such an amazing climber, his death was unthinkable. If this piece is imbued with a hidden melancholy, this is another of its sources.

EROS ON

THE HEIGHTS

That is no country for old men.
                —W. B. Yeats, "Sailing to Byzantium"

The UW Rock is the best of Seattle's fake rocks. Some
of the best, hardest, and most contrived bouldering in
the state.
                —Jeff Smoot, ClimbingWashington.com

For a while, a season or so, I met with Jeff Peters and Anderson at
the practice climbing rock at the University of Washington. This
was around 1976, and while the idea of climbing on buildings had
been around for some time, the idea of man-made structures designed for practice climbing was completely new. It was good for
me because at the time I was able to climb only on the weekends,
and many of them were rain soaked even on the east side of the
Cascades, where we often went. Also, it was good for me because I
possessed no real rock-climbing technique, only desire and endurance. I needed the practice.

Peters was a guy I worked with, older than me, a college graduate and a strong athlete. Anderson, his friend, was never referred
to by his first name. He was older still—mid-thirties, I would now
guess. Anderson was balding and had a bit of a paunch and a family, three conditions that I did not yet possess. All I knew was that I

wanted to climb. Anderson wanted to climb the Nose, the most famous rock climb in the United States, a three-thousand-foot route
on El Capitan in Yosemite Valley. I would be very happy to be able
to lead the last two pitches of Outer Space, a rock climb in Snow
Creek Canyon outside Leavenworth that had painfully revealed my
crack-climbing deficiencies.

Practice climbing might be more accurately described as a lot of
sitting around and speculating about the precipitation and wondering if the dog of the day, usually named Rasta, with a red bandanna
around its neck, could surmount the short concrete wall: "Hey, man,
that dog climbs better than you!" After this pseudo-climbing activity, we would repair to a pizza joint south of the U district and have
a few beers.

I remember one night Anderson shaking his head in amazement. "Look at this," he said, motioning with a twist of his neck to
indicate the whole of the dining room. "I don't know how you can
stand it." He was addressing me directly. "All this, this... pussy. Just,
just... here."

Political correctness had not yet reached the Northwest. Or us. It
was the young women, not the beer, that had reduced Anderson to
this state of inarticulation.

Unlike Anderson, I was hairy, svelte, young, and single, yet the
women in the room existed to me as if in a parallel universe. Unreachable. To quote Fitzgerald yet again, in our most eloquent novel
about desire, they were "as close as a star to the moon." As unreachable as the Nose. Astroman.

Anderson did not understand why I wasn't at this very moment
on my way to my Skid Row apartment with any of the obviously
available young women. The problem was, of course, that it was not
obvious to me that they were available.

Some time later I ran into Ray Smutek, who was Anderson's
brother-in-law. At the time, Smutek was the publisher of a climbing
magazine called *Off Belay*. I'm not sure what happened to him after

Off Belay folded in 1979, but he's credited with an oft-repeated line: "Time spent climbing mountains will not be deducted from your life."

I mentioned to Smutek that I had been climbing a little with Anderson; probably I didn't mention how little.

"Yeah?" said Smutek.

"Yeah," I said, "he's practicing for the Nose."

"The Nose." There was something in his voice, perhaps contempt. "Anderson is not going to climb the Nose." His tone further implied, "And you're an idiot to think so."

I knew immediately that Smutek was right. I had never questioned that Anderson would climb the Nose, but, no, of course, he wouldn't. This knowledge, the certainty of it, made me sad.

> You cannot stay on the summit forever: you have to
> come down again.... So why bother in the first place?
> Just this: what is above knows what is below, but what
> is below does not know what is above.... One descends,
> one sees no longer but one has seen. There is an art of
> conducting oneself in the lower regions by the memory
> of what one saw higher up. When one can no longer see,
> one can at least still know.
>
> —René Daumal, from the "Notes Found among
> the Author's Papers" in *Mount Analogue*

> Ascend to the terminus at about 6,500 ft. Climb to the
> head of the main portion of the glacier. The couloir is
> becoming broken up at the bergschrund base (7,800 ft)
> and melting out in its narrow part after early season.
> Cross the bridge to the largest schrund on the right,
> then the narrow upper schrund next to the rock on the
> right. Ascend snow-ice up the 50 degree couloir to its
> tip. A narrow portion at about midway is only 8 ft wide
> and in excess of 60 degrees (expect water ice here). The

final portion of the couloir leading to the West Ridge
notch (9,000 feet) may be eroded rock.

—Fred Beckey, route description of the Ice Glacier
Couloir in the *Cascade Alpine Guide*, Volume 1

Woody wore a cowboy hat, and his clothing smelled of woodsmoke. He drove a near antique BMW and generally let it be known that there were far too many people in the Puget Sound area and that he would be heading straight back to Wyoming as soon as he graduated. We met in 1976 in an undergraduate seminar in which Woody was studying Melville, and I was reading Coleridge. This was the course where I met the woman who would become my wife, a Wordsworth scholar.

I was going to go with some guys up to the St. Elias on the Alaska-Yukon border to do a climb that required a long approach on skis. Woody suggested that since I had never skied before, I ought to try it before embarking on a ski trip carrying a hundred-pound pack over seventy miles of glacial terrain that maybe had never been skied before. This seemed sensible, so I agreed to ski up the north side of Mount Stuart with him. Mount Stuart, in the central Cascades, is the largest nonvolcanic mountain in the state. As I recall, our plans were vague, but it also seems like Woody must have had a pretty good idea of what he, at least, was up to.

Woody did not have a guidebook; nor did he consult one. All his gear was well worn and looked to me like it came from another era. In Woody's presence I felt like a soft exile from the suburbs of the Midwest—which is exactly what I was. He was looking forward to using these skis he had found in a thrift shop and done considerable amounts of lathe work on, to the point that they appeared to have been engineered from rough planks of wood. Now they were works of art.

Soon enough I found myself skiing up a very steep couloir in very deep snow. I was on borrowed skis with new synthetic climbing skins, and there was ice on the adhesive, so the skins kept falling off. Woody had not dealt with synthetic skins before. He used wax to accomplish the same effect.

One of the old Swedes Peters and I worked with in Seattle had mentioned that, in the old country, semen was used on the bottoms of skis when wax was not available. We could never tell when he was joking or not, but one of the younger guys asked, "Where did they get it?" A moment of silence brought laughter from all, probably the point of the remark.

Woody stripped the skins off my skis and fashioned a set of faux skins out of knotted cord. I was impressed but still climbed at the frustrating pace of one step upward, two steps back. Also, having never skied before, I had not mastered the simple art of traversing a steep slope and making a kick turn to change directions. I was having a miserable time and working very hard at it. Woody had by now, skied upward and out of sight. But when I looked up, there was Woody skiing down to me in perfectly tight, evenly spaced turns through hip-deep powder. It looked as if he were auditioning for a Warren Miller film. Was I so pathetic that Woody carried my pack? If so, memory has mercifully blocked it out. Probably not—not because he wouldn't have been willing, but because he wouldn't have wanted to humiliate me by offering.

There was nothing to do but ascend. In truth, I was high enough now to realize that ascending was kicking my ass, but descending was likely to kill me. Woody rose out of sight again, and in a few hours I reached a snowy shelf where it leveled out. There, Woody was assembling blocks of snow into an igloo. As I was unable to stand, he directed me to scoot inside the foundation.

"I never said it was going to be easy," he said.

I absolved him of responsibility. By this time I was curled into the fetal position, and I stayed that way while the igloo took shape around me. Once out of the swirling snow—oh yeah, I forgot to mention that the weather had steadily deteriorated to the point that the igloo was finished in a whiteout—once out of the swirling snow, I began to pray that a helicopter might appear out of nowhere to pluck me to safety, depositing me, ideally, on my girlfriend's front porch.

The igloo blocked the maelstrom, and its interior was bathed in dim, bluish light. Woody fired up an antiquated Optimus stove and threw on a slab of bacon. I had never known anyone to carry bacon into the backcountry. My usual climbing partners favored unpalatable freeze-dried glop. We sopped up the bacon grease with sourdough bread that Woody had baked at home on his woodstove. This revived me sufficiently to begin plotting how to avoid reattaching myself to the skis.

The next morning we awoke encased in a cloud. I was eager not to descend, not possessing the skills to do so. So we went upward.

Woody picked a gully, and we climbed it, wondering after every pitch whether we should retreat. It was like driving in the dark on an unfamiliar road: we could see only to the end of the headlight beam. Before we could decide to bail out, we reached the west ridgeline of Mount Stuart, the end of our route, and looked over it to the peak's southern flank through the patchy white space. There wasn't much of a sense of triumph about it.

Later I would learn we had accomplished the first winter ascent of the Ice Glacier Couloir, a fact that, when presented to Woody, was met with utter indifference.

Once we got back to the igloo and loaded everything onto our backs, we clipped into our skis and began the descent, a long process that involved a lot of sliding on my butt and was generally softened by the depth of the snow. Back on flat ground we made another camp, knowing it would be a brief trip out to the car.

The next morning the weather was perfect, and we were filled with that euphoric sense of having performed some very private and deeply meaningful deed that would be incomprehensible to the larger world. We came to a Forest Service gate, took off our packs, and sat on them in our shirtsleeves under a blue sky, with a blinding sun reflecting off the white world. We opened a tin of oysters, the last of our food, and picked them out with the awl on my Swiss Army knife. These of course were a delicacy of unsurpassed sophistication.

We were goofy with pleasure, and Woody told me a story about an old cowboy, who, leaning against a gate as Woody was at this very moment, pronounced his general good spirits with a grinning proclamation now quoted by Woody himself, "Pussy Bueno."

We roared with laughter, because that seemed to sum it up so precisely.

But what had been summed up? That we were young men possessed with juvenile and sexist senses of humor? Hardly in doubt.

If desire is in essence a desire for wholeness, as the psychoanalytic theorist Jacques Lacan would have it, we attempt to close a "hole in the self" through an endless metonymic chain of supplements. The climber might fill the hole in himself by climbing; but as soon as the climb has been completed, desire moves onto something else—a woman, for example, the desire to be loved. Or, for the hard-core, the next climb.

> Through an infirmity of our natures, we suppose a case, and put ourselves into it, and hence are in two places at the same time and it is doubly difficult to get out.
> —Henry David Thoreau, *Walden*

> Few pieces of mountain architecture soar so grandly and prominently as this continuous sweep of ice, rock, and snow.
> —Andy Selters, on the north buttress of Mount Kennedy, in *Ways to the Sky: A Historical Guide to North American Mountaineering*

The longest I have ever been out was a trip from Seattle to Alaska that lasted, when all the traveling was added in, about sixty days. We spent thirty-five days in the backcountry and maybe three weeks traveling on the front end: driving up the Alcan Highway in a half-converted old school bus we had "won" with the minimum bid at a school district auction. We were stranded on the road for five days while three of us hitchhiked to Whitehorse with a broken-down transmission, and we waited for days clear enough to fly a food cache onto the glacier.

In retrospect, I understand that the climbing was potentially dangerous in this way: we were on our own. At the time, I can't remember thinking that it was particularly dangerous. We did not carry a radio, we had no prearranged flyovers, and we did not see any other party the whole trip. The only living things we saw were small finches that fluttered into our camp now and then. We also found their frozen bodies on the glaciers, huddled in little pockets of air just below the surface. Leslie Stephen discovered the same phenomenon in the Alps in 1873 and named his team's climb of the Grandes Jorasses the Hirondelles Ridge, the Ridge of the Swallows.

We had lots of food and fuel, and we knew how to extricate ourselves from crevasses. We knew to place our camps outside potential avalanche paths. I imagine now that we thought we knew a lot more than we actually did. We were young, reasonably strong, and did not expect to die.

Not expecting to die, I had two concerns on this trip: one, whether I would make the summit; and two, more important, whether the woman I loved would be there for me when I returned. A third concern hinged on the second: if she was, did that mean she was the one?

These first issues played out this way: despite about nine thousand feet of climbing over twenty-one days, I didn't reach the summit. Two of my friends were successful, and probably without my help they would not have succeeded. There was some solace in that.

We came out of the mountains feeling elated. I was anxious to return home, not only to solve the problems of my life, but because I was out of money. Alan and I hitchhiked from Haines Junction to Haines and caught the ferry to Seattle, sleeping under the canopy on the deck, eating the last of our expedition food and living off the kindness of strangers. At night the travelers drank and told their tales: logging, salmon fishing, mining, drinking—always that—and loneliness. Now we all were returning, triumphant, somehow, to whatever was coming next.

The three days passed in a hazy mist as the ferry floated down the Inside Passage, the effect being that we seemed motionless, and huge, slowly rolling murals of Asian waterscapes seemed to be perpetually rolled by giant, unseen hands for our viewing. Alan and I may have been out of money and food, but our fellow travelers were generous. We sat on the lounge chairs and read, of all things, climbing magazines, looking back or forward, I don't know. As it would turn out, I wouldn't climb again until the following summer.

The climbing expedition, all fifty-nine glorious days of it, had already become a distant blip in memory. My entire universe had become focused solely on my girlfriend, our reunion. Everything else had become insubstantial, dreamlike. The ferry itself, the *Matanuska,* seemed to have slowed to a state of watery suspension.

Finally, Seattle. The ferry terminal: there she was, standing on the heavily creosoted dock. I could see her expression, worried. That I wouldn't be there? That my love for her had been whittled away by the glaciers and the solitude and the sheer joyful work of it? In a single embrace she must have known I was back; I surely knew I was home.

We drove to another dock and we were ferried to the San Juan Islands and set about appreciating those things bestowed on those to whom a reprieve has been granted: we ate fresh strawberries, rode rented bicycles in the ocean breezes, and together plotted out our single future.

> This fella has a wild night with the boys at a strip club
> and comes stumbling home, drunk, lipstick all over
> his face and collar and smelling of cheap perfume. Just
> before he walks through the door, he dips his hands in a
> bag of climbing chalk hidden outside.
>
> His wife storms up. "WHERE HAVE YOU BEEN?! IT'S
> 4 A.M.!!"

The fella slurs, "I was at the strip club with the fellas."
"Bullshit, you were CLIMBING!!"
—Unattributed, off the Internet

A sardine tin would be sparsely populated compared
with that bivouac box, and we wondered whether the
unfortunate pair would come through the ordeal alive
enough to deal with Mt. Blanc on the morrow.
—Frank Smythe, on the bivouac hut on the
Col de la Fourche, in *Mountaineering Holiday*

The first summer I spent in Chamonix, I was climbing mostly with
my friend John. We had already been climbing together for nine
years, and since then we have climbed together for another quarter
century.

Beyond the problem of being scared to death of the Alps themselves, we had the additional challenge of John's traveling with his
girlfriend, whom I'll call M. The problem was this: we would go
climbing, and M would be in Chamonix on her own. Then we would
come back exhausted, having shared some near-vertical near disaster requiring a great amount of trust, not to mention luck, and the
actual physical connection of being tied together at the ends of a
165-foot piece of Perlon rope on which our lives depended.

One day when we returned from the heights, M had been out
hiking with some guy who tutored her in the history of alpinism,
a subject she had previously not shown much interest in. In retrospect it is easy to see that we ought to have taken a few days out of
our climbing schedule to do some walks in the Alps with her. I, of
course, would have been unnecessary to such a plan. However, I do
not recall this option being considered.

In Zermatt the weather was unsettled: new snow coated the Matterhorn, and no one was going up. In town we stayed in the Hotel
Bahnhof, which featured flowerpots fashioned from the climbing helmets of Japanese climbers who had not returned from the

heights. Also a communal kitchen in the basement and a dorm-style mass of cots in the attic. Like all mountain huts, this attic room was cramped and in need of better ventilation. It featured an older American climber with a vicious cough. It was hard to believe that his heaving would not crack his ribs.

Between hacks he spoke to John and me—probably, with M, we were the only other Americans up there. The guy sounded like he might expire any second, like this was a deathbed manifesto. God-dammit, he was here to climb these goddamned mountains and nothing was going to stop him. Hack hack hack. He was locked in a lifelong battle with these sons-a-bitchin' mountains, and goddam-mit HACK HACK HACK if a little coughing was going to get in his god-damned way.

Clearly, he should have been in the emergency room. We were left more or less speechless—like, yes, well, of course, we're here to climb, too. He was probably in his forties, younger than I am now. I remember looking at John and thinking, my God, is this where we're all headed? Looking back on it, I shudder to think what M might have thought about the scene.

The best climb John and I managed in the Alps was basically a retreat, but one of those that required an ascent to complete. We had ascended the *téléphérique* to the top of the Aiguille du Midi and then walked down its north ridge to the glacier, the Vallée Blanche, and headed over to the hut on the Col de la Fourche to attempt the Brenva Spur of Mont Blanc. Because we had bivied on top of the Ai-guille du Midi, we arrived at the hut early and had it all to ourselves for a few hours.

The hut had a kind of balcony that overlooked the Brenva Gla-cier, and we watched from it as a helicopter removed a dead body. We came to realize that one of the rucksacks in the hut must have belonged to the dead climber. This was unnerving. Meanwhile, the hut filled to beyond capacity. Amid dampness and sweat, coughing and snoring, muttering and packing up, sleep was impossible. And then the hut had emptied, so that by 2 A.M. we were once again its lone occupants. We were less than eager but finally rappelled down to the glacier and walked out to about the middle of it before admitting that the Brenva Spur was far beyond our skills and now, finally, beyond our desire.

Unsure whether we could climb back up to the hut, we devised an elaborate plan to gain the Brenva Ridge and follow it to the summit of the Tour Ronde, then descend back down to the glacier and up the ridge of the Aiguille du Midi to its summit from where we could catch the *téléphérique* back down to Chamonix. And we did just that, in a very, very long day.

I recall reaching the top and taking a photograph of a European climber apparently barking at the statue of the Blessed Virgin Mary that adorned the summit. Although my photographs are meticulously stored, I can no longer find that image among them, leading me to wonder if I dreamed it up out of hypoxia, dehydration, and dimming memory.

I do remember meeting up with some Brits as the day was nearly over; I felt ashamed that we had bailed off the Brenva before even setting foot on the route. But when we told the Brits what we did, they expressed amazement: "Well done! Brilliant!"

Sitting out on one of the decks waiting for the *téléphérique,* I met another Brit. He was sitting barefooted in the sun eating some dreadful concoction that he squeezed out of a tube. He had just soloed one of the big alpine routes—I no longer remember which— and was heading over to the north face of the Eiger. He had done the north wall of the Matterhorn earlier in the summer. His toenails looked like someone had taken a hammer to them, and his hair was almost matted. He was in some highly personal zone into which humanity did not venture often, though he was friendly enough.

During this era, I taught high school in southern California. I worked with Steve Levy, who, it turned out, was a kind of armchair mountaineer. He had done a little climbing, but not much, and we were always making plans that fell through at the last minute. Levy had been particularly enamored of Chris Bonington, having read the first two of his early climbing memoirs—Bonington's memoirs being a publishing enterprise unto themselves. I don't know what it was that Levy so loved about Bonington—perhaps just a distanced appreciation. Levy would ask me to tell him about the Alps, and I'd mention something. But his favorite image was of the lone climber up on the deck of the Aiguille du Midi. He was like a child insisting on a favorite bedtime story: "Tell me about that guy again."

Trying to arrange a climbing trip with Levy was impossible—he never came through. Later in life, after I had children of my own, I felt I understood Levy much better. I feel I owe him an apology.

The following summer John and M were still together. After they married, they lasted another six weeks or so. John, I believe, has been known to measure the marriage in days. That summer, 1981, John and I were planning to attempt a route on the east side of Mount Whitney. Unaware of the rigors of the approach, M decided to join us. I have written about this elsewhere, so I'll summarize briefly: there was an accident (not involving us), a very bloody head wound, and a helicopter evacuation. There was altitude sickness, vomiting, profanity and, from John and me, much laughter, prompting M's declaration: "Now I see exactly why you two BIG FUCKING IDIOTS love this so much." John and I tagged the summit via the Mountaineers' Route, and then, on the way down M, woefully underprepared in the footwear department, rolled her ankle and had to be semi-carried down to the car. In other words, a not untypical alpine excursion.

And though M left him after a few weeks of marriage, John and I manage to rope up together year after year.

> You can get what's second best, but it's hard to get enough.
> —David Wilcox, "Eye of the Hurricane"

If you are young and male, and your climbing partner is also young and male, and in addition he is single, he might not understand that for you, being married, climbing trips could become the source of, for lack of a better word, *tension* in your domestic life. Or maybe he did understand it, but simply thought that climbing shouldn't cause any such tension. Of course, it shouldn't.

That climbing partner was David Wright, and we climbed together a lot for a few years when we both lived in Salt Lake City. Once I went climbing with Wright and David Jenkins and Dave Bean. Most of our climbing was done in Little Cottonwood Canyon, which we could get to in a little over a half an hour. We also climbed in the Tetons, and at Joshua Tree and City of Rocks. This must have been over about a three- or four-year period, 1988–91. Whenever we crossed a state line out of Utah and into Wyoming or Idaho or Arizona, Wright would roll down the window and scream "Back in the USA!" Otherwise, screaming was very uncharacteristic of him. Before his father settled in Roswell, New Mexico, the family had done a stint in Utah, where the other children had mistreated young Wright for being non-Mormon. Yet here he was, back for more in his present incarnation as a graduate student.

Wright had an uncanny resemblance to an old friend of mine, and sometimes during long climbs I would refer to him in my own mind by the other person's name. Wright hated the wind, delivering a long bitter invective against it during a trip to Joshua Tree. On the drive back to Salt Lake we saw, spray-painted on the back of a road sign, the advice "NO CopS DRiVE LIKe HeLL." We did.

Despite his uncharacteristic rail against the wind, I remember this climb we were doing in Bell Canyon—the next canyon south of Little Cottonwood. I loved climbing in Bell's. Its access was, as I recall, a little squirrelly—you had to park in front of someone's house and then skirt carefully around private property. I can't remember ever seeing anyone up there. On this one climb, the wind blew up the dihedral we were climbing and took Wright's hat with it, blowing it seventy or eighty feet into the air, swirling it around, and then returning it directly to Wright's hand. The climb topped out on a ridgetop close to the mouth of the canyon, and to the west—it felt like it was just below us—you could see the whole grid of Salt Lake

City laid out in perfect seven-block-to-the-mile squares, the Great Salt Lake itself glimmering in the desert sun to the north.

Wright had been married briefly early in his life. He had been in the army, too. Worked as a carpenter. Despite the fact that he would soon have a PhD in English, he referred to women as "gals." We were in our mid-thirties when we found ourselves in graduate school. When Wright asked you to critique his work, he reminded you that "kindness is no kindness." He shot straight and asked for that in return.

Wright was telling me about this gal he had almost married. Probably we were descending some everyday climb, but it may have been that we were walking through the high desert at City of Rocks or bivied in a tent at the Lower Saddle between the Middle and Grand Teton. But let's say we had just summited one of the climbs in Bell Canyon and that we had just stumbled onto the bed of an elk, the cool dirt all but alive with the imprint of its body, and that we were now slip-sliding down a gully, all crampy-toed, sand spilling into our shoes.

We would have been reasonably confident that we could find our starting point, and Wright was talking about this gal he almost married. She was an artist, and they had been together two or three years, and all the impediments to marriage had been overcome. They were going on some hike, some high desert hike—Wright was from New Mexico—and they would arrive at this summit, and then Wright would propose, which was what was expected because, well, that's what it had come to.

The hike was going fine. Wright and the gal were seasoned hikers, companionable, they got along well. As they were approaching the summit, a woman was descending. Wright observed her scramble down a blocky section of rock. The woman was, according to Wright, perfect.

Perhaps I pressed for details of this perfection: "Perfect?"

He could add no details: only that she was a vision. Perfect. Nothing more. Maybe he glimpsed the line of muscle on her calf as she descended past him. But that was it. He had glimpsed perfection, and now, he knew, it would be impossible to marry his gal.

Wright did not propose, and their relationship ended soon after.

I try to keep this episode in mind when Wright shakes his head at my wife's silence as he and I pack for a road trip to City of Rocks.

> The eternal feminine draws us on high.
>
> —Goethe, *Faust*

> Snake Dike became the most popular climber's route to the top of the most spectacular hunk of granite in North America.
>
> —Steve Roper, *Yosemite Valley Free Climbs*

One time we were doing this route on Half Dome in Yosemite. Even if you have never entered Yosemite Valley, if you know the works of Ansel Adams, you probably know Half Dome. Its northwest face makes it look like a sphere cleaved in half, and much of the technical climbing is on this face—all of it beyond my reach, I can now sadly be sure. A hiking route has been constructed on the east slope, its gentlest. Handrails of steel cables have been installed. These are rough on the hands, and at the beginning of the handrails is a pile of leather gloves for hikers to don, of particular use during the descent. Even this hiking route entails a sixteen-mile round trip.

In between the cable route and the famous blank Northwest Face there is another blank wall and also the Southwest Face, on which there is a route theoretically within our capabilities: Snake Dike.

A stout hike in finds us at the base of Snake Dike in about four hours. That is, in the vicinity of the base of Snake Dike. We see no signs whatever of the beginning of a climbing route. Further, the wall is large, scarily large from John's point of view. He sits in the dirt and states that no way is he going up, even if we do find the route. To think that he could do a climb of this scale was sea-level folly.

We go over to this spot called the Diving Board that sticks out over the valley. It's the kind of thing you lie on and inch up to the edge until your head is at the end and it feels like you're suspended in midair, and the view is, of course, sensational. Probably the hike was worth it simply to experience this.

Then some people appear and start up Snake Dike, and we no longer have the excuse of not knowing where the route starts.

I persuade John to rope up, and soon we are cruising because that's the kind of route it is, made for moving fast. The end of the climbing comes soon enough but leaves over a thousand feet of slabs to hike to the top. The face is in dead-on afternoon sun, and the rock is baking. We save perhaps a swig of water, but no more than that, for the summit.

I have heard stories of enterprising folks carrying ice and drinks to the summit. But had they actually appeared, would we have had money on us? We are parched, and it is later in the day than we had expected it to be. It has been one of those days when everything is on schedule and no time is wasted, but nonetheless the middle hours of the day seem to have disappeared somewhere—into a huge vat of hours that won't be deducted from our lives, we hope.

At the summit there is something of a circus atmosphere. More people than you would think are on top. Later, after descending the cables, I am shocked that so many folks brave them. There is a popular gift shop T-shirt that says *I Climbed Half Dome*; these folks have earned it.

As we approach the summit, a young woman in a day-glo halter top passes us. I might not remember this if it hadn't been for John, who comes out of his dehydration death throes, the ones he experiences often as we summit, and says as if from beyond the grave, "I will never get over that."

I know what he means. Exactly.

The thing is this: women may not draw us to the heights, but they often draw some of us, one way or another, back down from them.

ON CLIMBING THE SIERRA MATTERHORN
AGAIN AFTER THIRTY-ONE YEARS
Range after range of mountains
Year after year after year
I am still in love.
—*4.x.40086, On the summit*

—Gary Snyder

Chestnut Mountain Resort: "Ranked among the top 10
midwest ski resorts by *Ski* Magazine."
—Chestnut Mountain Trail Map

When the weather is borderline in Chamonix and you decide to go up anyway, up the *téléphérique*, the cabin rises straight into the clouds, and for a few minutes you are not so much on a climbing trip as being transported through space.

At Chestnut Mountain in northern Illinois, the rise is far less dramatic. In fact, when you step out of your car into the parking lot, you are at the "high point" of the resort. From the lodge you ski down—475 vertical feet, they proudly remind you—to the bottom of the runs, where a fence keeps you from the railroad tracks that separate you from the Mississippi. Higher mathematics is not required to calculate the ratio of time spent on a lift to the time skiing the runs. At Snowbird in Little Cottonwood Canyon above Salt Lake City, I remember skiers measuring the intensity of their days by the number of tram rides they made to the top of Hidden Peak, from which a 3,240 vertical descent takes one back to the tram. The number of tram rides multiplied by the vertical descent equals the day's total skiing.

At Chestnut it's never crowded when I ski. Usually it's the last week of the season, and you can ski right to the chair; there's rarely a line. I figure to make six or seven runs an hour. Mostly I'm riding the lifts by myself. My kids are somewhere on the mountain, the terrain park probably. We find each other off and on during the day, usually when they need money—which in truth is not often, because they won't stop until I make them, which is when the lifts are closing. Their goal clearly has nothing to do with maximizing their runs. All they care about is getting "air." Probably if they were anything like me, they would calculate the number of minutes they spent per day with their boards airborne. One of my goals is to keep the surface of my skis on the snow at all times.

I am talking with a friend about the appointment of someone to a prestigious academic position. My friend worries that the new appointee lacks the gravitas of her predecessor. I knew what he meant, but *gravitas*? Is that really the condition toward which I am directing my energies? I hope not. *Air.* Maybe my son has the right idea: pursue air. The salary of someone possessing gravitas—that's another story.

At Chestnut the lifts are rarely very far off the ground, which is littered with dropped gloves, poles, tubes of lip balm, and the occasional beer can. But raising one's gaze from the ground, in the branches, fluttering in the wind, are three brassieres, two black and one red.

I have to confess I like the idea of it: girls of a certain age, a dare, a bet, a night of wild skiing. Who knows what it might mean? Shoes laced together and flung over the power lines, staking out the territory of youth.

Wordsworth wrote: "My heart leaps up when I behold / A rainbow in the sky." Pretty safe. "My heart leaps up when I behold / a bra hanging in the trees" doesn't quite match it for poetic occasion.

What I was really feeling was my age. That the world in which young women might fling their bras into the trees from the chairlift is one that I left so long ago I can't even recall it. It's probably more accurate to say it's a world I never really visited. You couldn't reach the bras with your ski pole, that's for sure: they're about as close as a star to the moon.

2008

I hope that there is no sense of self-pitying in this last piece. The tone of it feels now to me like that of a finished man looking back. I feel much less finished now than I apparently did at the time I wrote this. And yet, I am always very conscious on the last day of ski season that I must live in the moment, that next ski season may never come.

At some point the Cascade guidebook announced that the first winter ascent of the Ice Glacier Couloir on Mount Stuart had occurred a year earlier than Woody and I had been on it. And, who knows, it could have happened much earlier and gone unreported; after all, we didn't report our ascent.

THE TOWER AND
THE RIDDLE

What walks on four feet in the morning, two feet
at noon, and three feet in the evening?

I. MORNING

March 1975: I was leaving the Midwest in a battered AMC Javelin
that easily held all my possessions, with a Bottecchia bicycle, worth
about as much as the car, lashed to its roof.

I didn't hate Detroit, or my family, or my life there so much as
I had simply noticed that what I was living for was the times I was
away from there. Now I was on my way to Seattle, a destination I'd
chosen sight unseen.

Dave Johnston and I were caravanning in our separate cars. He
was an agreeable guy: although he wasn't a climber, he nonetheless
agreed to detour off I-90 to have a look at Devils Tower in northeast
Wyoming. This was before *Close Encounters of the Third Kind*, and before Steck and Roper's anointing of the Durrance Route in *Fifty Classic Climbs in North America*. These sources of fame would come soon.

In *Close Encounters* Roy Neary, the everyman played by Richard
Dreyfuss, is summoned to the Tower—the aliens have called him
there, right? Or did the Tower call the aliens? In any case, the iconic
peak was imprinted in his brain: he was called there, away from his
job, from his family, from the world as he had known it. Called to
higher things.

How exactly I came to be called to the Tower—the moment of im-printing—I can't now remember, but that I had been called to higher things there was no doubt.

I'm not sure if N. Scott Momaday is right about the Tower stirring "in the hearts of men an awful fear." I know it stirred in me a desire to climb it. The "awful fear" part didn't creep in until after I had com-mitted to do so.

The campgrounds were not at all crowded this early in the sea-son, and it didn't take long to notice a pair of rugby-shirted guys sorting gear and strike up a conversation. I myself owned a rugby shirt, identifying me (in my own mind) as a member of their tribe. I also owned a Whillans sit harness, a rope, and a climbing helmet. None of these items had been overly used yet, particularly not on rock climbs.

Eventually I got up the nerve to ask if they would add me to their partnership. Had I been more experienced, I probably wouldn't have asked. Had they been more experienced, they probably wouldn't have said yes. But they did say yes, and thus began a sleepless night, prefiguring David Byrne's slap to the forehead: "My God! What have I done?"

Both guys were named Mark, they were from New York, regu-lar climbers at the Shawangunks, and this would be their longest climb. Breakfast was a soft Snickers bar and a lukewarm cup of tea that tasted peculiarly of the aluminum in which the water had been boiled. Details like this I remember precisely; others are fuzzier, probable reconstructions, guesses.

Although there was no guidebook, the Marks had studied the route at the ranger station. Features of the route were named: the Durrance Crack, the Cussin' Crack, the Jump Traverse, and the Meadows.

The climbing was difficult for me, in my full-sized mountain boots, and I have edited out of memory the number of times I asked for tension. I'm assuming it was not a rare request. It goes without saying that I didn't lead a pitch.

One of the photographs the Marks were kind enough to send shows me sort of flopped out at a belay, too hammered to sit up straight, the look in my eyes that of prey in the jaws of a fierce predator.

The summit was a revelation: a meadow in the sky, and I was ecstatic to be there. A sign on top said "No Climbing above This Point." We thought this sign was the coolest thing ever. An in-joke that we had earned. That's how young we were, and also how early in American climbing this was.

Getting down became problematic. As we pulled down the rappel rope, it became hung up, more than once. Many time-consuming machinations were required, and we had been out of water for hours when we reached the deck in the near darkness.

There we encountered a mightily pissed-off ranger. He was pissed for two reasons: one, I was not officially registered for the climb, and two, one of us (the ranger wrongly assumed it had been me) had climbed without a helmet. He wasn't just "don't let it happen again" angry; he saw our crimes as a deliberate personal insult, a flouting of his authority that should earn us a lifetime ban from climbing in the park. It was unbelievable.

Soon the tongue-lashing abated and we were at a restaurant, toasting ourselves in the glow of fellowship and ascent. In the morning Dave and I would resume our westward migration. I was filled with exhilaration beyond belief: three days out of Detroit, and I had climbed Devils Tower.

I didn't care that I hadn't led a pitch, wasn't embarrassed by how much tension must have been required to keep me upright and ascending. Didn't care about my role in the mini-epic descent. These aspects would only occur to me much later.

The new world, the one I was making for myself, was alive with possibilities, and I was here, now, ready to grasp at whatever might be slightly out of my reach.

II. NOON

The year was 1988 or '89, and the occasion is harder to reconstruct than the first climb because it lacked significance: it's a single climb in a blur of activity, long past. I was in the middle of a six-year stint as a graduate student in Salt Lake City, where I devoted hours every day to running and climbed regularly.

By then we had sticky rubber soles on our climbing shoes, spring-loaded camming devices to protect against falls, and chalk to improve our grip. Despite these advancements, the rating on the Durrance Route had somehow risen; now it was rated 5.7, even though no single move exceeds 5.6. The argument was that sustained 5.6 somehow equals 5.7. No matter, or, as is now ubiquitously observed: "Whatever."

I was climbing with my long-standing partner, John. We had been released from our long-standing commitment to the Grand Teton to explore a bit, having finally, on his fourth attempt over many years, succeeded on its famous Exum Ridge. All we needed was cooperative weather. What I didn't realize was how far Devils Tower was, exactly, from Salt Lake City. I was too cool to do more than glance at a map.

In the middle of the night we were only to Rawlins, which was dark and seemingly deserted and which we were quick to judge a wasteland. In my memory, we listened to a single tape, Tracy Chapman, which ultimately I decided only made me almost as depressed as she seemed to be. We arrived at the Tower about noon, racked up our climbing gear in the parking lot, and set off.

Because I'd told John that the approach was short, he was wearing something called "driving moccasins." But the approach wasn't that short, although the trail around the base of the Tower had been paved in the years since I had first visited. Because I had been climbing a lot, the climb did not particularly inspire or scare me. What an idiot I was: it should have done both.

As we flaked the rope for the first pitch, we heard the unmistakable jangle of hardware that can only denote a leader fall, followed by a litany of curses. We waited several minutes to discover the fate of the fallen.

First the ends of the rappel line reached us, and shortly thereafter the fallen leader, sporting a shoulder that had been yanked out of its socket. His feet had slipped, but his hand jam had held. Something like that, anyway. He managed to make the rap, but his eyes were beginning to glaze. We waited for his partner to arrive before we started up.

At this point in our partnership, I had a lot more vertical miles on my odometer than John did, and sometimes I overestimated his abilities, desires, and general level of fitness. It was no longer necessarily true that he could follow anything I could lead. The climb isn't really that long. I would know at the top of the second pitch whether John would be able to make it.

The Jump Traverse, which I had been dragged over fourteen years earlier, was now something I simply stepped across on lead. I would have been hard pressed to say what the crux of this climb was. Hard pressed to admit that it even had a crux.

In the photographs, the sky is not cloudy all day, and in many, John is flashing the thumbs-up sign. "What's wrong with that guy?" one of my friends would ask later, on viewing the photos. But I just remember being relieved that we could do this thing together, that it was epic-free, and that the weather would hold. It was, after all, by this time, one of the fifty classic climbs in North America. And yet we had the line and the summit to ourselves.

III. EVENING

Late summer 2009: I am driving across the country and north to Alaska with my two sons. We are on a strict timetable, scheduled to rendezvous with friends in Montana and having to stick the landing for both guys on the first day of school. But I wanted them to see the Tower, and it wasn't that far out of the way: we were on I-90, after all.

Although this was strictly a no-frills excursion, we splurged on breakfast just outside the gates of the park. They both wanted to climb the Tower, but it wasn't in the cards: we were off to Montana, and I was sad because frankly I didn't expect I'd pass this way again, ever. We lived in Anchorage now, and there was plenty to do in our own backyard. Devils Tower was off the list.

Late summer 2010: against all expectations, we were doing the five-thousand-mile drive again. The previous year had been rough in some ways. The boys hadn't been speaking to each other for the previous eight months. We are (long story) in two cars, once again a caravan. This year, however, we have both the time for the climb and a pair of ropes for the rappels.

The guys are pretty decent, but not passionate, climbers, and the older one has put in a lot of time in the gym. He boulders at about V6, which is medium hard. He can clip bolts on bolt-projected climbs. Neither of them can lead a traditional, unbolted climb.

We're on the route early enough, the weather somewhat threatening. We are doing the pitch below and east of "the first pitch," the one that starts where the last rap lets you off the face. In other words, we had botched the approach and added for ourselves an extra pitch. At first I think I'm going to just scramble up it, and then I put in protection, and then it begins to feel kind of hard, at least harder than I had expected. Macklin, the younger, comes next, and he struggles mightily, suffering from some recent basketball or skateboarding back ailment. His yowling en route I take as preliminary to his announcement that he's bailing. Dougal, the elder, follows faster than I can reel in the rope.

"No way," Macklin says. "I'm outta here."

This is an announcement that can only be honored. But the truth is, I wanted to do this with the three of us. I wanted the work and play of the climbing to heal the rift between them, and I was deeply saddened as Macklin rapped off. I wondered if Dougal and I should continue. It wouldn't be what I had envisioned, and it wouldn't be a good thing to have excluded Macklin, even by his own choice, from the summit.

Dougal and I scrambled over to the proper belay spot for the first real pitch, and I began thinking how hard it had been for me that first time, thinking about the guy with the out-of-socket shoulder. I was thinking how fit I had been twenty years earlier and how I didn't really want Macklin to feel any worse than he obviously already did. (Later, I would find out that he had just days earlier broken up with his longtime girlfriend.)

We flake the rope, I shoulder the rack, and I walk up the little ramp to where the business begins. It's steep, but not very far to the belay. I put my hands in the crack. Vertical. But it's only 5.5, if I remember correctly. And it's not very far. But I'm thinking about Macklin, his long walk all the way back to the campground. And, it's true, I'm thinking about the extra twenty pounds I'm carrying—one for each year since my last ascent. Dougal's carrying the extra rope, and I'm thinking we probably climbed it on double nine-millimeter ropes the last time. I make a couple moves upward and look at the dark clouds to the west. I hear in my mind the words of John Menlove Edwards, arguing with himself fifteen feet off the ground while soloing: "Get down therefore."

"I'm not feeling it," I say to Dougal, and I climb back down to him and explain myself, somewhat less articulately than I'm doing now. What I'm really feeling is: *I just don't have it anymore.*

We're kind of quiet on the rappel, as I basically conclude that I have just chickened out on a route that in my mind should have been easy, *had* been easy the last time I did it. But face it: it's twenty years later, and I'm not the same guy, not really.

I think hard about the previous year. On the plus side, I had done a lot of skiing. There's not a lot of rock climbing around Anchorage, and it's easier to do other stuff—skiing, mountaineering, even bicycling. The year before, I had spent a lot of dark winter nights in the gym, and the previous spring in the Alaska Range I had led some pretty hard stuff. But I just didn't put the hours in this last winter. At my age it's not exactly like riding a bicycle anymore.

Bottom line: I'm feeling my age, a feeling I've been able to ignore pretty consistently up to now. I think of the riddle of the Sphinx: here I am, leaning on my imaginary cane, three-footed in the evening. I know the answer to the riddle that Oedipus answered—not that it did Oedipus any good. And I know it now in a different, less clever, way: personally, through experience. It was not enough for poor Oedipus to answer the riddle of the Sphinx; he went on to fulfill his dark destiny, or, if you prefer, to suffer the consequences of ignoring a divine warning.

I suppose that this time I heard the warning. But the warnings are *always* there, aren't they? "Get down therefore." How many times have we heard it? There's a Sphinx on every mountain, and it well might devour us if we don't answer the riddle wisely. We learn and relearn when to heed and when to carry on every time.

I'm planning to carry on, three-legged into the night.

2010

Two after-the-essay stories: first, after the piece appeared in *Alpinist,* one of the New York Marks wrote to the editor and identified himself. Still climbing and living now in Colorado, he confirmed that his memory of the climb was pretty much the same as mine; second, when my son Dougal read this, he was horrified. "You told the whole world we chickened out on Devils Tower?" Whoops. Were it only true that the whole world reads *Alpinist.* The route is now high on his tick list.

LIVES OF THE

VOLCANO POETS

who disappeared into the volcanoes of Mexico leaving
behind nothing but the shadow of dungarees and the
lava and ash of poetry scattered in fireplace Chicago
                                        —Allen Ginsberg, *Howl*

It was natural to think of this line from *Howl*, referring to the mysterious poet John Hoffman, on hearing of the equally mysterious disappearance of the poet Craig Arnold on a small Japanese volcanic
island in April 2009.

Hoffman, a Beat poet from before they were beat, died in Mexico
in 1952 at age twenty-four in unknown circumstances, his body cre-
mated among strangers. His devoted friend, Philip Lamantia, read
Hoffman's poems at the famous Six Gallery reading of 1955, which
also featured Gary Snyder, and, of course, Ginsberg reading "Howl."
The event was thinly fictionalized, as well as immortalized, by one
of the audience, Jack Kerouac, in *The Dharma Bums*. At the time of
his early and curious death, almost none of Hoffman's poems had
been published, but Lamantia produced from his "effects" a slen-
der volume called *Journey to the End,* published for the first time in
2000. Ginsberg's "volcanoes" were figurative, but Hoffman's death
was not.

More is known about Craig Arnold. Older than Hoffman, Arnold
nonetheless died young, at only forty-three. He had published two

volumes of poetry to great acclaim: *Shells*, a Yale Series of Younger Poets selection, and *Made Flesh*, just a year before he went missing. Arnold and I attended the same graduate program, barely overlapping in our courses of study, he coming and me going; and although we were acquaintances, not friends, he was known already to be a rising star, and I followed his career from a distance. Once his disappearance had been noted, briefly and cryptically, on the Internet, I became entranced with his story, following it moment by moment in real time until the final search-and-rescue team concluded that he had had some sort of accident and fallen into a ravine. His girl-friend issued this statement: "His trail indicates that after sustaining a leg injury, Craig fell from a very high and very dangerous cliff and there is virtually no possibility that Craig could have survived that fall." The search for his body was abandoned as too dangerous. Identification of his tracks had been confirmed by his footprints: earlier in his journey he had photographed his own footprint in lava.

Arnold was studying volcanoes for a poetry project, and he kept a blog titled *Volcano Pilgrim: Five Months in Japan as a Wandering Poet*. Reading the blog with the arguable advantage of hindsight, one can't know whether Arnold's attention to death is prescient or simply a poet's natural attention to the largest issue. He made four entries on April 26, the day before he would hike into forever.

One of the entries, "Myakejima, 3," begins: "You feel like you are seeing everything now. Nothing was happening, and now everything is happening. Why does your sight seem now so sharp and clear?"

The same entry ends: "Danger has a way of cutting through melancholy, the real fear blinding you to the fear dimly imagined. If you could only always just have escaped death, you would never be sad again."

It must also be true—at least I hope it is—that if you *don't* escape death, you'll never be sad again either.

Perhaps the last words he wrote conclude entry 4, from April 26, and describe the smell of the *ashitaba* leaf when it is crushed in the hands: "It is the smell of a world in which there is nothing rotten or putrid or sulfurous, a world in which all those things have been rinsed away."

The search-and-rescue team was careful to clarify that Arnold did not fall into the crater of the volcano but into a ravine.

My own interest in volcanoes began at an early age. In the third grade I became obsessed with geology. Part of the attraction was that I believed we lived in a geology-free zone, a Detroit suburb. Our neighborhood had been bulldozed down to near bedrock and built up again. The developers planted a lone maple in front of every house. Everything else had been scraped away, as if scoured by an Ice Age glacier.

I collected rocks and identified them from books. I began to look at the bigger picture. The diagram that I found most compelling was a cutaway of a volcano. This was an illustration from the 1950s, and it looked like the cutaway drawing of a human heart, the roots of a giant oak, or the chambers of hell.

During the bus ride to school, I was talking to an older kid I barely knew about my interest in geology. He couldn't believe it: they were studying geology in his sixth grade class that very day. Somehow it was arranged, based on this kid's enthusiasm for my apparent knowledge, that I should come to his class and tell them about volcanoes. I didn't particularly want to do this, but I was flattered by the attention. I knew the terms *magma, lava, vents,* and *fumaroles.* All that stuff. Even, rabbit out of the hat: *pyroclastic flow.*

But the nun whose class I was visiting was not happy. These were Felicians, a stern bunch in the early sixties. She wanted to know *why* the volcanoes erupted. I thought I had covered that: molten lava, pressure, building pressure, *voilà*—eruption.

No. She wanted to know why the core of the earth was molten. Why it erupted.

I started to repeat myself, pressure, etc.

"No," she said, "you don't know."

This produced a feeling I would recognize many years later during comprehensive oral exams in graduate school.

She thanked me curtly and sent me back to the third grade, ears burning. Thus ended my short career lecturing on geology. Only now do I realize what she may have wanted. She wanted the theological explanation: Hell.

I lost interest in geology but found it again, sort of, when I became interested in topography, in the form of mountaineering. The first large mountain I found myself on was Popocatépetl, the volcano, snow-covered then, that hovers over Mexico City with its equally imposing partner, Iztaccíhuatl. If you go to enough Mexican restaurants, you will eventually see a mural of these two peaks: Popo, the smoking warrior, and Izta, the sleeping lady.

The fifth highest peak in North America. The rim of the summit cone revealed a deep crater with a tiny blue lake at its bottom. Sulfur leaked from various vents in the snow, and its summit, like every other summit I reached in Mexico, was adorned with an iron crucifix.

I left Mexico intending to return as soon as possible, which turned out to be two years later. On this venture I traveled alone, with no itinerary but to visit the tops of as many mountains as possible. I was now twenty years old. My idea was to write a guidebook to these mountains, and thus I considered my travels "research." I found a book in English called *Under the Volcano* by Malcolm Lowry. It was an edition that was not available in the United States and said so on the cover, which featured the muralist Diego Rivera's *Day of the Dead*. At the time I naively thought it was unavailable in the United States because it had been censored, a forbidden book. I was wrong, of course. I learned that although I was reasonably well prepared for the climbing I had planned to do, I was not at all prepared to read Lowry, which did not appear to feature the volcanoes, or not very much.

One of the more memorable events of the whole excursion occurred high on Iztaccíhuatl when I became a victim of food poisoning and altitude sickness, resulting in the hallucination that a demon was sitting on my chest with the sole intention of pinning me to the mountain forever. I was able to shake him off, but my subsequent wandering, shoeless on the glacier, led to frostbite, and I was lucky to make it down to the hospital in Mexico City.

Later, when I was ready for Lowry, I found there these lines: "From these mountains emanated a strange melancholy force that tried to hold him here bodily, which was its weight, the weight of many things, but mostly of sorrow."

One of Lowry's few specific mentions of the volcanoes comes in the novel's final scene, the death of the main character, the consul, Geoffrey Firmin, in which he hallucinates that he is ascending Popocatépetl: "He trudged the slope of the foothills alone. With ventilated snow goggles, with alpenstock, pockets full of dried prunes, and raisins and nuts . . . and now he had reached the summit. . . . But there was nothing there: no peaks, no life, no climb."

The hallucination continues with the sense that he has indeed ascended but is falling into the crater. In fact, his monumental drinking binge ends in a cantina, where he is shot and unceremoniously dumped into a ravine. The novel ends with a dead dog being thrown in after him.

Lowry himself did not live to fifty. The coroner described his end as "death by misadventure," by which he meant a lethal combination of alcohol and sleeping pills. Lowry wrote, "I love hell. I can't wait to get back." The fact that the words were spoken by the consul, in a novel, is sometimes elided from the attribution. And yet Lowry also wrote, "He was glad that the man was interested in his life, since this was indeed interest in his work at one remove." A writer is sometimes his own best fictional creation.

Popo erupted before the turn of the century, its snowy dome melted away. It remains closed to mountaineering.

The first section of Gary Snyder's book *Danger on Peaks* is a personal history of Mount St. Helens described over a lifetime of familiarity.

Snyder's style is, as is well known, a form of spiritual autobiography deeply rooted in the natural world. His first ascent of the peak was on August 13, 1945. He writes of making what he calls his "summit petition to the shapely mountain, 'Please help this life.' When I tried to look over and down to the world below—*there was nothing there.*"

Returning down to Spirit Lake after that first climb, Snyder read the news of the atomic bombings of Hiroshima and Nagasaki, the estimated 150,000 dead, and the declaration by an American scientist that "nothing will grow there again for seventy years."

And yet Snyder visited Mount St. Helens after the devastation of the 1980 eruption, where, out of the firestorm and ash, life there had found its way: "One final trip before leaving, a walk to Ghost Lake: pearly everlasting, huckleberries and fireweed, all the way."

I think of his poem "A Berry Feast," the poem he read at Six Gallery, the night of "Howl," the night of Lamantia's revelation of John Hoffman's foreshortened genius. "A Berry Feast" ends:

> Dead city in dry summer
> Where berries grow.

Before it erupted in 1980, Mount St. Helens was an almost perfectly shaped snow cone. Only a learned eye could distinguish its photograph from one of Fujiyama, the sacred mountain of Japan. I consider myself lucky to have climbed it in its perfect platonic form, in 1975, five years before the pyroclastic event.

Despite the intervening years, I remember details of the ascent well. John and I had driven down from Seattle after dinner with the intention of climbing the Forsythe Glacier the following day. But we arrived late and wired and spent a few sleepless hours in our overly warm sleeping bags before we decided to just head up under the light of a fullish moon. The summit was a revelation—a huge flat, filled-in crater. Who would not be moved to prayer, all the world spread out at our feet, Mounts Hood, Adams, and Rainier shining on the horizons, treasure houses awaiting our arrival?

In geologic time, of course, five years is a single historic moment. It's as if the eruption and our standing on the summit occupied the same drop of water on the back of a whale.

Natural disasters seem to be prevalent in these post-Katrina days, with a vague, unspoken nod to end times and possible ecological karmic payback in the form of global warming. Geologic disasters, though, are on a different order from climate-based disasters. Recently Indonesia has been ravaged by the eruption of Mount Merapi. One of the many casualties of the eruption was Mbah Maridjan, the volcano's spiritual gatekeeper, appointed to the position by the sultan in 1983. He refused to leave his home despite government-ordered evacuations. His charred body was discovered in an attitude of prayer, and he was buried next to the previous gatekeeper, his father. He was eighty-three years old.

Maridjan seems a sort of shamanistic figure, a strange spiritual remnant from an earlier century when sultans ruled and spiritual gatekeepers were government appointees. And yet, when Mount St. Helens went in 1980, so went Harry Truman, the longtime caretaker of the Spirit Lake Lodge. People who knew him surmised that he never expected he wouldn't have time to evacuate. He now presumably rests under 150 feet of volcanic landslide debris at the foot of the mountain with his 1956 pink Cadillac, sixteen cats, and untold amounts of loot, some perhaps left from his bootlegging years, or accrued more slowly in his fifty-four years of proprietorship of the lodge. Truman, like Maridjan, was eighty-three years old at the time of the eruption.

I have been on Mount Rainier more times than I've been on any other mountain. I last climbed it in 2006, thirty years after my first successful climb. Every ascent is a gift, but this climb was particularly memorable, and not just because my friend John finally reached the summit for the first time after a couple early failures. The year before, I had been diagnosed with cancer, which, though successfully surgically removed, nonetheless took an unexpected psychic toll—by which I mean I hadn't expected the disease to fill so much of my consciousness. Mount Rainier was the first mountain to which I returned after the surgery. The ascent was uneventful, just the way you want it to be while you're climbing, though that doesn't make for much of a story afterwards.

We hit the crater rim early enough in the morning and trudged across it toward the summit, which is on the south side of the rim. The path in the snow was nearly a trench at this late point in the season, and on the way we passed another group already returning across the crater toward the descent route. They raised their gloved hands and one by one high-fived me as we passed, and I found myself overcome by emotion. I have stood on many summits and felt giddy on them many times (depending on how severe I expected the descent to be). But I don't think I ever wept before. And I realized that I truly hadn't known if I would ever climb again, if I would experience this grandeur again. In fact, I wasn't sure I would be alive at all. But I was here, now, and I felt I had been granted a great reprieve. For one crazy, hypoxic moment I thought I was walking though the gates of heaven.

In his timeless, unfinished metaphysical adventure novel *Mount Analogue*, René Daumal posits the physical existence of the ultimate mountain, the point at which earth and heaven meet. Daumal had been living in the mountains for his health and had been learning alpinism; his notes on climbing, a mere four pages in total, are included in an afterword to the text and are as illustrative of the art as anything that has ever been written. The text proper ends mid-sentence, as Daumal died of tuberculosis at the age of thirty-six before he could finish. Among the notes was the title for his final unwritten chapter: "And you, what do you seek?"

His wife, Véra, who assembled the book for publication eight years after his death, notes that this is a "more disturbing and fruitful question than the numerous stock answers made to it, a question each of us must finally answer for himself."

Daumal must have known that it's not the object of our seeking, the grail, but the seeking itself that is its own answer.

Surely, these volcano poets were, or are, all seekers, though who among them has said what exactly they sought? Hoffman left fragments; Lowry left us long, mysterious riddles of rich narrative prose. It seems a safe assumption that Truman and Maridjan, fixed for eternity on their home mountains, had found *something*. As I write this, a sultan in Indonesia contemplates the appointment of the new spiritual gatekeeper of Mount Merapi, poets take up their pens, and climbers tie themselves into ropes, preparing for ascent.

T. S. Eliot observed that when we come to the end of our exploring we arrive where we started and know the place for the first time. Then there are those of us who, so caught up in the chase, never return. Others of us are lucky to know that we occupy home and away, heaven and hell, the mountaintop and the plain all in a single moment. It's too much, easily forgotten. Remember then to crush the *ashitaba* leaves in your palms and breathe deeply, pick the huckleberries. As Snyder says, the natural world speaks to us: "'New friends and dear sweet old tree ghosts / here we are again. Enjoy the day.'"

As *you* prepare for the ascent, be careful in choosing to whom you listen.

2011

At the time I wrote this I had never hiked in mountain jungles of a rain-drenched Pacific island with deep ravines on two sides. Now I have done so and can more readily see how a solo hiker like Craig Arnold could slip into oblivion on a wet day.

HERE COMES
OL' FLATTOP

In the dozen or so times I climbed Flattop last winter, we didn't see any other hikers. In summer the Glen Alps parking lot might be filled, and all manner of hikers make the pilgrimage, including sandal-shod kids, miniature yapping dogs, and an unusual number of semi-invalids. More power to them. It's the closest peak to most of Anchorage and more or less the easiest.

In winter it's a different encounter: weather, a sliver of danger, and solitude, the very qualities I seem to value, if history is any measure. On Dimond Boulevard, one thermometer says 6 and the other −6. But it's really about the wind. Erich's car is good on ice, and he's screwed bolts onto his soles like old-fashioned Tricouni. Winter mornings are not dark, exactly: there's light in the sky but no sun, and the snow has an eerie, bluish glow to it, as if the whole enterprise is being conducted in some netherworld time zone.

Once we leave the frozen road for the frozen trail, we're moving single file, and conversation is over. Usually we climb at our own pace, spread out over hundreds of yards. This day Erich, Bill, Dave, and I keep close. Every few hundred yards we huddle together to ask if we're still doing this. Apparently we are. Upward, each in a separate universe of wind and icy footing.

The last five hundred feet have too much snow to find what might have been a trail. No one has been here to leave tracks, and it's been too windy anyway. We're all wandering up, more or less randomly. The gusts are strong enough to knock you off your feet if your balance isn't perfect. The wind is blowing ice under my glasses, which are fogged with my breath, and pretty soon, the wind *does* knock me to the ground—all right, I just lose my balance—and I'm crawling, sort of blindly, up the mountain. I remember a film version of *Lear*—Russian—Lear crawling over the moors, bewailing his fate in universal moaning and English subtitles. I feel like this, except for the wailing part. Probably I'm not wailing only because I'm reasonably confident I could crawl all the way back to the car if I had to.

The wind stops for a beat, and the whooshing I hear, I realize, is my heart pushing blood through my body at a manic pace, thundering in my eardrums. Above us the wind has blown a hole in the sky, and I see that on Peak 2 someone, a lone skier, has made a dozen perfect turns down the otherwise untouched west face. Man, I think, that's a lot of work for a dozen turns.

Then I realize that I'm probably working harder than the skier was, yet I will not soon get the pleasure of making those twelve perfect turns. I must be doing it for some other reason. And it's not about the summit, a place I have been dozens of times in all possible conditions. I am slow to arrive at the obvious, and, yes, I know it's a cliché: this is a form of daily practice, each step its own reward.

2010

Though I record the occasions I climb Flattop, I have never counted them. It's certainly over fifty. Most of the climbs have been done in the company of the same three guys: Erich Heinrich, Bill Myers, and Dave Ward, and usually joined by a small crew of canines: Eleanor and Curzon, for sure, but sometimes Libby and Hyde, and now Zia.

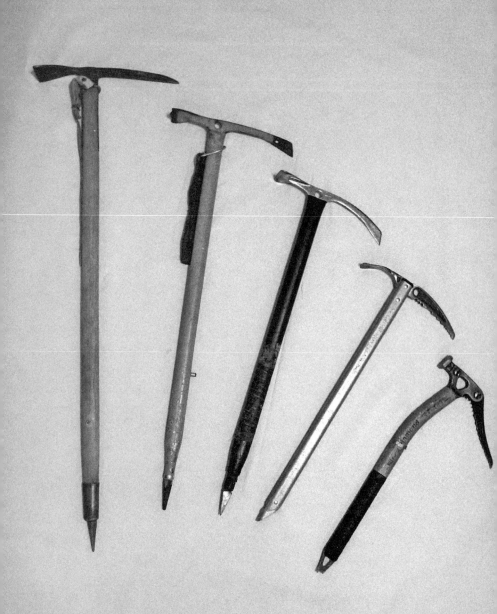

A SHORT CULTURAL HISTORY OF THE ICE AXE IN THE TWENTIETH CENTURY

> There seems to be a great variety of opinion amongst
> Alpine travellers as to the best form of alpenstock. Every
> man, of course, is attached to his own theory; and it is as
> dangerous to criticise a man's alpenstock as his sonnet.
>   —Leslie Stephen

Leslie Stephen wrote the first treatise in English on the ice axe in the *Alpine Journal* in 1864: "The Best Form of Alpenstock for Use in the High Alps." This was the Leslie Stephen who was founding editor of the massive *Dictionary of National Biography,* recording twenty-nine thousand lives. Eminent Victorian literary critic. Early president of the Alpine Club. Author of *The Playground of Europe,* which, along with Edward Whymper's *Scrambles amongst the Alps,* celebrated the golden age of the Alpine climbing and sent generations of Brits to the continent, in search of . . . something. Still, Stephen is largely forgotten, except as the father of Virginia Woolf. From there, it's a short leap to Mr Ramsay, the fictional tyrant of *To the Lighthouse.*

The golden age of the Alps, by the way, is an early blip on the timeline of alpinism, beginning in 1854 with Alfred Wills's ascent of the Wetterhorn and ending a scant eleven years later with

Whymper's famous ascent of the Matterhorn. Two ironies here. Wills only *thought* he made the first ascent of the Wetterhorn: actually it had been accomplished ten years earlier. And common lore has it that Whymper's ascent started an era, not ended one. The "golden age" is used loosely and arguably to describe the era following the foundation of the Alpine Club in London in 1857, when Brits began pursuing first ascents in the Alps with the not inconsiderable help of local guides. During the golden age, Stephen made ten first ascents of Alpine peaks, always in the company of local guides, who he believed were three times better than the best amateur.

Guided climbing went out of style for a long while just after Stephen's generation, except in Chamonix. Today guiding is becoming fairly common again. This revival is due, I think to relatively wealthy novices, coming to the activity late in life and wanting a shortcut to bagging trophy peaks. The first to do the Seven Summits (the highest peak on each continent), Dick Bass, had a nice vision, but it's hard not to ascribe a lack of imagination to those who follow him. This is an aside in a piece that will ramble much, even outside the asides.

In Stephen's day, one of the primary purposes of the axe was to cut steps in steep ice faces. This technique became passé when crampons were invented and perfected. For Stephen, cutting steps was the guide's job, not something he would deign to do himself. "I must take here the liberty of observing that I do not myself ever cut steps when I can get a guide to do it for me, first because a guide can do it much better, and secondly, because he is paid to do it."

In this respect Stephen was basically out of step with today's values. In other ways he was ahead of his day. He believed that the chief end of climbing was climbing—not science, not research, but climbing for its own sake. This decidedly nonutilitarian philosophy of climbing was criticized by others, notably John Ruskin, who was outraged by Stephen's lighting a pipe of tobacco on the summits of peaks, as if this pleasure were decadent and somehow at odds with the noble enterprise and serious business of climbing. Stephen was fond of drawing, and one of his little sketches is of a monkey sitting in a tree smoking a pipe. This may speak to any number of strands of Stephen's thought: Darwinism, for example, or merely human folly. One imagines Stephen, the happy animal on the summit of one of his many Alpine conquests, contentedly smoking the celebratory bowl.

Stephen began his observations on the alpenstock with two central tenets, both of which remain true today:

1. It must be strong enough.
2. It must not be unwieldy.

Stephen might be surprised to learn that an alpinist today may own, as I do, a whole quiver of axes. My first was acquired in 1971 and is made out of aluminum. The great alpinist and tool designer Yvon Chouinard once referred to this very tool as a "day-glo metal monster for snow slogging." In fact, of the x number of axes I own, (including hammers), only one has a wooden shaft. My current favorite is the Grivel Air Tech Racing Light. It weighs less than a pound. It is also short: there is no trace left of its ancestry, the walking stick. It is strong and easily wielded, but without heft. It was once too light for the unexpected task at hand, which required something akin to chopping steps. Stephen would probably not deign to pick his teeth with such an unsubstantial instrument, for, as he says: "Every Alpine traveler however, will agree that it is useful to have some instrument capable of cutting steps on emergencies, as when you find yourself on a glacier alone, or your guide breaks or loses his axe."

When Stephen used the word *Alpine* he capitalized it, because it was at that time a literal term referring specifically to the Alps. Used in this context today the word is still appropriately capitalized. However, today it is often lowercased as a generic term for "mountains." Interestingly, though, an *alpinist* today is a practitioner of the particular art of mountaineering. This distinction is due partly to the specializations within the activity. Lito Tejada-Flores delineates several such specializations in his well-known essay "Games Climbers Play" in 1967. Since then even more areas of specialization have appeared, including gym climbing.

An alpinist today might be a kind of elitist, as opposed to, say, a *sport climber,* referring to a rock climber who protects the climb by clipping the rope into preplaced bolts, or a peak bagger, who often walks to the tops of peaks or is guided up peaks of limited technical difficulty. The Canadian satirist and cartoonist Tami Knight self-deprecatingly refers to "alpinists" as "owl penises." Self-deprecation as a character trait in mountaineering may indeed have begun with Leslie Stephen—the monkey in a tree, smoking pipe in hand. This tone is evident somewhat in George Mallory: "Have we vanquished an enemy? None but ourselves."

But Stephen had a more hallowed sense of the Alps. His conception of climbing considered the Alps as some sort of platonic form of mountains and mountaineering, an ideal against which every potential rival mountain range fell short. When Stephen read Martin Conway's 1894 account of an expedition to the Karakoram, his "review" in the *Alpine Journal* considered the mighty Karakoram as a mountain range inferior to the Alps in every aspect except height.

And although I have not climbed in the Karakoram (unlike Stephen, I would like to) I have made three pilgrimages to the Alps, and Stephen's point is well taken: what more does one need? And, of course, new challenges continue to be found in the Alps, even though the last of the six great north faces, on the Eiger, was climbed in 1938.

One of Stephen's last climbs was Mont Mallet, also known as the Aiguille Noire point of Mont Maudit. In fact, he had already retired from "the fanaticism which made me regard it as a solemn duty to spend all available moments of leisure in measuring myself against some previously inaccessible peak." He unretired to climb Mont Mallet for enjoyment.

From the top of Mont Mallet, after his party "indulged in frantic howls," Stephen lit his pipe and contemplated the view, including the "astonishing pinnacle" of the Dent du Géant, which he surmised might be ascended someday "with the help of rockets and a sufficient allowance of rope." He and his party collectively agreed: "Nobody will ever get up that peak by fair means." He concluded this meditation by reiterating, "If anybody, by fair climbing ever reaches the summit of the Dent du Géant, I can only say that my ideas of the capacities of human nature will be materially enlarged."

One then wishes to know if this indeed was the case when, eleven years later, in 1882, the Dent du Géant was indeed climbed by three members of the Maquignaz family and company. Perhaps Stephen questioned the "fair means" by which the party spent four days fixing ropes with pitons prior to the ascent. Or perhaps this would be an argument for another era. In any case, climbing for Stephen was over.

When Gaston Rébuffat compiled his *Mont Blanc Massif: The Hundred Finest Routes*, he listed the routes by increasing difficulty. The Dent du Géant comes in at number 33: in other words, two-thirds of the climbs he lists are harder. One wonders how much Stephen's capacity would be enlarged by the thought of Rébuffat's climb number 100: the Central Pillar of Frêney on Mont Blanc.

Stephen died in 1904, thirty-three years after his climb of Mont Mallet. In the same year, Colonel Francis Younghusband invaded Tibet and claimed Lhasa for the British Empire, *Peter Pan* opened on the London stage, and in New York City, Robert Oppenheimer was born, who some forty years later would describe himself with words from the Bhagavad Gita: "Destroyer of worlds." Also in 1904, R. L. G. Irving, author of *The Romance of Mountaineering* would take a promising seventeen-year-old schoolboy, George Leigh Mallory, on his first visit to the Alps.

And the alpenstock, how would it fare in this new century? It was already gone, having evolved into the more sophisticated piolet, or ice axe, midcentury. In 1889, the young Italian priest Achille Ratti probably used a Grivel on his ascent of the Dufourspitze thirty-three years before becoming His Holiness Pope Pius XI. In Mexico City in 1941 the young Stalinist Ramón Mercader would strike the exiled Leon Trotsky in the head with an ice axe, leading to his death. In 1953, high on K2, Pete Schoening would employ the famous single-axe belay that held five of his living partners and the body of Art Gilkey. His axe is enshrined in the American Museum of Mountaineering and accompanied by a single photograph of the families of the men whose lives he saved.

I don't know who put the DMM Predator in Stephen King's hands, any more than I know how it was Mercader arrived at the ice axe as his weapon of choice for political assassination. The Predator is a short axe designed specifically for ice climbing in the late 1990s. King announced famously, "I look at the DMM Predator and I think of murder." Of course, any number of objects might set him off like that. But he looked more closely and noted in the May 2004 issue of *Outside* magazine: "There's no part of the axe that doesn't work, from the rough-hewn butt-end with its wrist-loop strap to the arched line of the handle to its wicked, burrowing tip. . . . What I really feel when I hold this in my hand isn't so much the possibility of murder as the gravity of mortal things. It speaks to me of the vulnerability of human flesh, but also of the resilience and determination of the human mind."

And old Leslie Stephen, a footnote to literary history by his own self-fulfilling prophecy, what would he think of the DMM Predator, climbing two-fisted with leashless tools, dry tooling? All he wanted was a walking stick he could cut steps with, if his guide should prove unable to do so. Of the thousands of pages of writing he published, Stephen's own favorite piece was "Sunset on Mt Blanc." The definitive biography of Stephen, Noel Annan's *Leslie Stephen: The Godless Victorian,* runs to 436 pages. Of these, a scant eight are devoted to climbing.

Annan writes, "Each of us, however gentle or wasted our life, has a place in history, usually as the nameless representative of some class or status group or movement." Stephen may be a footnote, but when he had to, he swung that alpenstock and carved out an ascending path of steps, that many of us, tools in hand, continue to follow.

2011

This concept began as plan for a series of fictionalized stories about ice axes in the hands of historical people: Leslie Stephen, Pius XI, Leon Trotsky, and Vladimir Nabokov. Year after year I didn't write them and ultimately the concept boiled down to this essay, sans Nabokov.

THREE DREAMS
OF MOUNTAINS,
LATE FALL 2004

SHIPROCK

We're going to climb a mountain, John, Tama, and I.

But John is not well, so we're wheeling him around in a shopping cart. The cart has a simple platform built on it on which a tent is set up, and John is bivouacked inside, talking with us unseen through the nylon walls.

We're pushing him on asphalt sidewalks of the sort that wind through golf courses for motorized carts. People are walking, strolling, on the paths as in a Seurat painting.

We push the cart toward the mountain, and the mountain, I now realize, is Shiprock.

We stop to look up at it, and I think, "Am I ready for this?" This hasn't occurred to me before, but does now, with reference to my recent cancer, surgery, and recovery.

YOSEMITE

I have a problem: how will I get both of my cars from Yosemite back home to Los Angeles?

There is a reason both cars are here, but I cannot summon it to consciousness.

I walk to the hot tub. As I approach, there is Aisha, whom I did not expect to see in Yosemite. Her hair is cut short, and I tell her it looks nice and reach to touch the back of her neck, remembering at the last second that I ought not to. We embrace, and I now realize that we are wearing wetsuits. This, we both understand, is for the best.

We have not seen each other for years—it's as if this were a second lifetime. Aisha is worried about the reception of the new book she has written.

Nonsense, I tell her, there is no reason to worry.

But, she says, I read a chapter of it in public and the audience was mean.

I tell her they were just jealous little snots, believing she is consoled by my stock answer.

I am a bit preoccupied with the issue of how to get this second car back to Los Angeles, but I don't mention it to Aisha; her driving it is not even in the realm of possibility. This, I tell myself, is my problem.

LAKE LOUISE

We are skiing, Roy and I, down a steep, bumpy, east-facing slope.

When we get near the bottom of the slope, I cannot stop, and I ski right into the lake. The lake is not ice covered, though chunks of ice float on the surface like miniature icebergs. I am standing about ten feet off the shore—my momentum has carried me this far. I am chest deep in the icy water, and my skis are still on. This is Lake Louise, I now realize, and the western shore sits under the east face of Mount Victoria, far from humanity.

I can't get the skis off, and the bank is too steep for me to side-step up to shore. Roy cannot pull me out. This is out-of-bounds skiing. There is nowhere to go for help, nowhere Roy could reach in time. I will die soon of hypothermia. Roy and I both understand this.

2004

The John referred to in the first section is my friend John Mann, not the otherwise pervasive John McInerney. John Mann and Tama Baldwin are close friends and poets. John joined Dougal and Macklin and me on a great climbing road trip west, the occasion of the climb recounted in "Axe of Contrition."

Chuck Pratt wrote of Shiprock in *Ascent* in 1970: "Shiprock, fabled monument, rises before us in splendor and silence, a tableau from the genesis of the Southwest, historical remnant of a unique volcanic violence which has created a collage of mountainous fluted columns, jagged aretes and sheer orange walls that intimidate us into silence." I have never been to Shiprock.

Roy Plaeger-Brockway was my climbing partner and best friend circa 1976 and 1977. We never skied together.

WHILLANS,
HASTON,
AND ME

A Distanced Appreciation with a
Couple Trip Reports, Contextualized

In the prologue of Jim Perrin's biography of Don Whillans, *The Villain*, the author describes Whillans and Dougal Haston's groundbreaking 1970 ascent of Annapurna and ends with the sentence: "From Annapurna's summit, it only remained to go down."

Haston's memoir, *In High Places* ("an autobiography, of sorts," Perrin says), ends before his success with Doug Scott on Everest in 1975, and Whillans's memoir, *Don Whillans: Portrait of a Mountaineer*, with Alick Omerud, ends between the climb on Annapurna and the invitation to join an Everest expedition in 1971.

Perrin seems to take Whillans to task for not maintaining his place at the top of the mountaineering world. But how long can anyone maintain such a position? Haston had a good run, to be sure. Even so, it lasted only about seven years, from the summit of Annapurna to his untimely death.

Since my father's name is Dougal, it is my middle name, and my firstborn son is Dougal as well, it is not surprising that I was interested in Dougal Haston from the time his name first appeared on my radar screen in connection with his Annapurna climb with Whillans. Haston was the first person I knew of outside our family who shared our name, a name that means, my son reminds me, "dark stranger."

Thus in the summer of 1976, when Haston and Doug Scott came through Seattle on their way back from Denali, where they had put up a new route on the South Face, my friend Roy called me up on the phone. He could do this only because we were both at work—neither of us owned telephones in our Skid Row apartments.

"Haston and Scott are here," he whispered. "Can you get over here?"

I couldn't. "What are they saying?"

"Scott's doing all the talking. Haston isn't saying anything. He looks ... far away."

And that was as close as I got to meeting Haston: talking to my climbing partner on the phone while Haston was sitting in the same room. He would be dead within a year, even before his and Scott's trip report of their Denali climb appeared in the *American Alpine Journal*. Unbelievable.

I think about the chilling irony of Haston, who, within days of finishing his novel, which features a scene of a skier outrunning an avalanche on La Riondaz, goes out and skis the very terrain as his character but is overtaken by an avalanche and killed. Haston granted his character the reprieve that fate would not extend to him. The novel was posthumously titled *Calculated Risk*, though what Haston would have called it we don't know.

Jeff Connor, Haston's biographer (*The Philosophy of Risk*, 2002), speculates that Haston's scarf, a rakish accessory, may well have been the cause of his asphyxiation. This caught me off guard. I had already known about the strange coincidence of his dying on the same slope that his character skis just hours after he finished writing. I wrote the following trip report as a record for my sons, a what-not-to-do-next-time kind of accounting, and it holds another coincidence:

Tin Can Ridge, November 14, 2009 (one day after Friday the 13th)

We're heading to Turnagain Pass for some early-season skiing. Running late, 12:30 P.M. It's about ten degrees under perfect blue skies. Christian, my son's friend, is a fourteen-year-old skiing savant and has supplied the road tunes: the Arab surf music that Tarantino uses to begin *Pulp Fiction*.

From the car we can see the trail up Tin Can Ridge. It's after two o'clock. We're boot packing. The hike is a little longish, steep in places, and, well, just longer than I had anticipated. I'm thinking of a turnaround time of about 4:30. The sun has just about set when we get above treeline and there's no way to get lost, right? We pass a couple we've been sort of leapfrogging back and forth with, and they're on their way down. "What's the latest we should start down, d'ya think?" I ask. "Five, no later." But why listen to them? They're starting down now! We'll just follow our trail back. A couple thousand feet down, but on skis. We're talking minutes. So we press on.

Above the treeline the light is "glorious," according to Macklin, and Christian spots a place to build a ramp. Since he's ahead of Mack and Dougal, he sets to it, and it takes them almost a half hour—could it be that long?—to catch us. By the time the ramp is done, the sun has definitely set, but to ski the ramp Christian, Macklin, and Dougal have to ascend another three or four hundred feet. I realize I completely misvisualized the project, thinking they were going to hop down just twenty feet and do some easy early-season jumps. But no, this thing requires a humongous approach, and the idea is to launch oneself into the stratosphere, high enough for Christian to do a 720 corkscrew, which I can't actually picture but believe to be something quite serious.

Christian launches first; he's coming at me like a hellbat, but as he hits the launch zone, the snow slows him way down, and he hits the ramp with just enough speed to plop over the lip like a dud firecracker. Macklin and Dougal are somewhere out of view. Taking their ole swweeet time. Later they will say their hands were too cold to fasten their bindings. Macklin comes down like a sensible person, cruising the slope, back and forth. Though, of course, were any of us truly sensible we wouldn't be here at all. Dougal heads down, also hellbat style, barely in control, not even aiming at the ramp. His hat flies off, and his scarf is trailing behind him. He barely holds on until the snow brings him to a stop. Then Dougal and Macklin have to come up to where Christian and I are standing for one last view into the twilight before we head down. I'm still on the two-thousand-foot-descent-in-about-fifteen-minutes plan. Easily done . . . on a groomer at the resort.

It's too dark to really see the trail. *We're just going down, right?* Dougal and Macklin disappear down an untracked, powder-filled gully, which heads, disturbingly, northward instead of westward and back to the car. Christian disappears into the trees at warp speed, basically toward the line of ascent. I split the difference. Within minutes I am launched into the powder, ejected from both skis, and generally starting to worry. To get the general tenor of the rest of the evening, repeat that last sentence four or five times.

I find my skis, work my way through the trees, find myself cliffed out. Flounder in the deep snow and continue generally downward, with no real certainty of compass direction. Floundering around in the dark, deep snow in subzero temperatures, one naturally thinks of Jack London's story "To Build a Fire." The verb *flounder* cannot be repeated enough. No, I mean, one naturally thinks of one's children and how one has led them to their. . . . No, one naturally thinks of one's general unpreparedness and the fact that the car can't be too far off even if it will be an utterly miserable business to find it.

Finally I reach level ground. I take off my skis and begin wading through waist-deep snow. Suddenly, through the alders, here are Macklin and Dougal and Christian, miraculously together.

We are now moving slowly, with some confidence, toward the road. Dougal breaks down a little, starts retching miserably. I send Macklin ahead with Christian (to whom Macklin rightly refers as a Zen master). I give Dougal a steaming cupful of hot cocoa, of which I have two thermoses, reserved, apparently, for just this eventuality. Dougal discovers that his scarf was wrapped around his neck in some bizarre hangman's fashion and that he was strangling himself with every step. Thus replenished, we trudge out the final fifteen minutes to the car on terrain that looks utterly foreign and unlike anything we had approached on.

At the gas station at the Girdwood turnoff, I buy twenty bucks' worth of junk food. The attendant says to Dougal, "Hey man, you've got a tree in your hair." The artifacts of a good bushwhack.

On the drive home Christian says, "I kind of remember now, that's what happened to us the last time too." Halfway to Anchorage, Dougal grabs the bag of potato chips and pukes into it.

I remember a day of salmon fishing on a charter boat; I had been horrifically seasick the whole trip and had sat in the cabin with my head on the table, my face in a puddle of vomit. As the captain steered back into the harbor I lifted my head for the first time in hours, and this little old man with a twinkle in his eye took note and said, "And a good time was had by all."

When we got home, Macklin was without his hat, and one of Christian's ski poles had disappeared. My watch, too, had mysteriously disappeared from my wrist. When we dropped Christian off, his mom met us at the door. "Did you have fun?" she asked. It seemed an innocent question.

"It was great!" we all agreed, neglecting to add how happy we were to be alive.

"Glorious," Macklin concluded.

In the tale of two scarves, fate would grant my Dougal a reprieve that Haston allowed his character but that fate would not grant him.

I can't say that this means anything at all. The only lessons I derive seem to be the old ones, a continual reminder to be careful. Apparently I need them. Still, one can't help thinking that "there are more things in heaven and earth, Horatio, than are dreamt of in your philosophy."

The summer that Haston climbed Denali, Whillans also climbed Denali, by the West Rib. Perrin takes Whillans to task, describing him as "plodding up the Western Rib—one of the straightforward *voies normales* to Denali's summit." Don was one of nearly five hundred climbers in eighty-five teams on the mountain. Haston and Doug Scott, by contrast, were on their new route, and other Brits were on the Cassin Ridge, doing the first alpine-style ascent. Perrin notes that Whillans was forty-three, but that Riccardo Cassin himself at the time of his eponymous route was fifty-two. Perrin adds the harsh observation: "In mountaineering terms, what remained was simply leftover life to kill," echoing his opening chapter's conclusion: "From Annapurna's summit, it only remained to go down."

But the West Rib of Denali is not quite the *voie normale* that Perrin would have his readers think. In fact in 1976, only twelve climbers summited by the West Rib—the exact number of successful climbers on the Cassin that season.

As *The Villain* and Whillans's life wind down to their final pages and months, the list of activities Whillans participates in seems to work against Perrin's argument. "Mount Aspiring in New Zealand with Bob and Anne Schneider" Perrin dismisses in a single sentence. Whoa! Bob Schneider. I know Bob, have roped up with him (okay, in the gym), and I can't remember his ever mentioning Don. I check with Bob, and sure, he was also the lone American on the West Rib climb, in addition to accompanying Whillans on Mount Aspiring. I play the "chain of ropemates" game. My son Dougal has roped up with me, I've roped up with Bob, Bob has roped up with Whillans, and Whillans with Haston. Thus we go from Dougal to Dougal in five degrees of separation.

For all Whillans's supposed villainy, he never did anything near approaching Haston's darkest moment. Haston, as a young man driving under the influence, hit a group of pedestrians, one of whom died. And then he ran off, eventually spending sixty days in jail. Yet Haston is always the rock-star cult figure, the brooding philosophy student; Whillans is the brawling hooligan.

My favorite anecdote in Perrin's book has to do with Whillans and Perrin himself (Perrin rarely figures in the book; it's not that kind of biography). When Perrin's biography of John Menlove Edwards came out, Whillans approaches him "drunk and aggressive" and says, "What's all this yer bin writing, about J. M. Edwards bein' a fuckin' queer?"

Months later, Whillans took Perrin aside in a pub and offered an olive branch. "'I read yer book,' he started, fixing me with narrowed eyes, face breaking into a smile. 'I think there's one or two things in there you might regret writing in twenty years' time, but yer did a good job.'" On this occasion, Whillans—legendary, according to Perrin, for never buying a round—bought the drinks. As Perrin says: "The generosity of it, the considered delivery, the graciousness of the implied apology, were utterly heart-warming. It was the last contact I was to have with him."

I wonder what Whillans would have thought, not only of the actual biography about him but about the idea of such biography. I can't help thinking he would have preferred to be left in peace, as was his hope for the Abominable Snowman, which he believed he saw on Annapurna. Chris Bonington, in *Annapurna South Face*, allows Don an extended monologue on the yeti sighting. It ends with Don's "If it's managed to survive so long and under such bitterly cold conditions, it deserves to be left alone."

Whillans on Haston: "It's as though he were behind glass. You can see him but you can't touch him." You're getting this from me, and I got it from Perrin, who got it from Ingrid Cranfield, and who knows how many degrees of separation between Cranfield and Whillans himself.

And for the opposite view, Haston on Whillans, think of the summit photo Haston took of him on Annapurna. It's as blurry and inconclusive and, well, useless, as any photo in our photographic history, and yet for all its fuzziness and artlessness the moment is captured: "Whillans on the summit of Annapurna, which he and Haston reached at 2 P.M. on 27th May 1970."

Haston was thirty-seven years old in 1977, when the avalanche caught him—the same age as Whillans in 1970, when the pair summited Annapurna. Haston died very close to the height of his powers, frozen in time as well as space, suspended, as it were, in midlife, as surely as figures on Keats's Grecian urn: "When old age shall this generation waste / Thou shalt remain."

It occurs to me that Whillans must almost certainly have started his first ascent of the Central Pillar of Frêney on Mont Blanc, with Chris Bonington, Ian Clough, and Jan Duglosz, from the Col de la Fourche hut. (Clough's death on Annapurna "ruined the triumph" for Whillans.)

Sure enough: "The hut was only sparsely populated and we cooked a leisurely meal and then turned in to enjoy a few hours' sleep before our early start. On the back wall of the hut, a large coloured picture, torn from a magazine, showed four happy climbers posed in the hut door: Guillaume, Vielle, Kohlman and Mazeaud; three dead, one still convalescing."

Guillaume, Vielle, and Kohlman had died earlier in the summer attempting the same route in one of the "most catastrophic saga of postwar alpinism," judges Perrin, (who, by the way, apparently finds Whillans's account of the hut quite reliable, repeating it nearly verbatim in *The Villain*!). The sentiment among the French climbers present was that the first ascent of the route should be reserved for the French, out of respect to the valiant climbers who perished in the storm. But Whillans and company got there first, a full day ahead of René Desmaison and company.

My own memory of that hut remains vivid despite tempering by nearly four decades.

First season in the Alps, we thought we were going to do the Brenva Spur on Mt Blanc (Ha!). Caught the last téléphérique up the Aiguille di Midi, bivied semi-legally (okay, *illegally*) in the tunnel up there, got an early start to the Col de la Fourche and found ourselves the only ones at the hut. A party had left a couple packs there. We had all afternoon to lounge around and look across the glacier at the Brenva, getting more intimidated by the minute. Late in the afternoon a helicopter came in and retrieved a body from the glacier; presumably the climbers had fallen from Mt Maudit, and, logically, had stayed at the hut, their abandoned packs sitting in the corner. Sobering as hell. The hut filled way beyond capacity and in the middle of the night we rapped off the hut railing down to the glacier from which the Brenva loomed ever larger in the moonlight. At some point we realized we were in way over our heads and started on Plan B, which, of course, didn't exist. We climbed back up to the ridge the hut was on and traversed it over to the summit of Tour Ronde. Basically we were just looking for a way to get back to Chamonix. We tagged the summit and zombie-trudged back up to the top of the Aiguille di Midi, caught the last 'phérique to Cham and shortly were hoisting pints at the Bar National—this was back before it became gentrified. At the time we felt like hard-spanked losers, but in memory probably my favorite 48 hours in the Alps. The Brenva for a while after that was known death route due to falling seracs and was rarely climbed. I've since heard it's come back into shape again. Climbed Mt Blanc with the same partner over twenty years later.

That's a basic trip report, with a flourish or two, written for another occasion. It leaves out what I really best remember: finding a pair of crystals on block on the ridge, the sense that no one had ever climbed on this ridge (because, well, why would you?), the summit of the Tour Ronde (by no means a foregone conclusion), the strange French climber barking at the statue of the Virgin Mary at the summit, and then, on the way back up to the Aiguille du Midi, a group of British climbers amazed by our little detour: "You did *what*?" and us feeling for the first time that, okay, maybe we did something after all.

But the strangest thing on that climb was what happened when we sat on the glacier in the middle of the night, having just given up on the Brenva and trying to figure out what to do next. It was dark, we couldn't really see much, and we were sort of stalling for daylight. We could see on the map what we thought we might do, but couldn't really see enough of the ridge to know if it were even remotely possible. We were warm enough, so we sat on our packs and waited. From behind the ridge to the east, a bright light appeared from some unknown source in the sky. Unimaginably bright—we were stunned by it, and it was getting brighter, though we couldn't see its source. It had to be a UFO. Cavemen witnessing an eclipse, the shepherds watching the angels announce the birth of the Christ child. Within minutes a full moon rose over the ridge and lit the whole glacier in a preternatural light. The moon! Unbelievable. But of course. What the hell else would it be? Idiots!

In *Don Whillans: Portrait of a Mountaineer*, Whillans describes his bivy on the ridge after his first ascent of the west face of the Aiguille de Blaitière with Joe Brown:

> The clouds had cleared and the night was magnificent, still and starlit. I clipped myself on to the ledge and dozed off. I awoke to find Joe already awake, cursing and shivering in the cold. A point of light on the horizon cheered us up and we watched eagerly for the appearance of the sun. The light grew stronger and we were laughing and talking like normal human beings when suddenly the moon popped up.
>
> "Hey—that's—what the—n, bloody hell, no," stuttered Joe in dismay.
>
> We spent the rest of the night in utter misery until the real dawn arrived.

In Whillans and Brown I find comforting precedent for not distinguishing the approaching moon from the sun or some other, less natural source of illumination.

Perrin characterizes *Don Whillans: Portrait of a Mountaineer* as "highly unreliable memoirs," which I can only surmise means that while researching *The Villain,* Perrin found differing accounts from the ones Whillans recounts. Remember Perrin's appraisal of Haston: "An autobiography of sorts."

Gaston Rébuffat, in his resplendent classic *The Mont Blanc Massif: The Hundred Finest Routes,* says of the hardest climb, the Central Pillar of Frêney: "The most obvious aspect of this route is the physical and moral commitment that it requires. Other routes present greater and more sustained difficulties, but none demands such powers of decision and exact mountaineering judgment, this because of the remoteness and the difficulty of retreat in case of bad weather." First ascent: Whillans, Bonington, Clough, and Duglosz, 1961.

Moral commitment. In the end, I appreciate Whillans more than ever, and what to make of Dougal Haston, dark stranger? I haven't seen many photographs of the two of them in the same frame, but one notable shot by John Cleare from Camp 4 on Everest in 1971 shows Whillans, his goggles pulled up onto his hat, a lit cigar clamped in his mouth, and Haston breathing from a bulky oxygen apparatus with dark sunglasses over his eyes.

Although Haston left us with three books, I can't help feeling that the mask never came entirely off. In the apparently fictional *Calculated Risk*—which, incidentally, would have had to be much revised had Dougal survived to do it—the hero's early speculation may reveal more of Haston than his nonfiction does: "Where will I be in another five years—or maybe at the end of next week: a penniless corpse at the foot of a crevasse, remembered only in climbing guide books and pubs where I drank twenty pints and walked out?"

But Dougal himself wouldn't make it to the end of next week. We don't know on which day exactly he wrote these prescient words:

"That evening Jack was aiming for the summit of La Riondaz, whose steep face provided one of the best runs of Leysin, although it was often out of shape due to avalanche danger."

I told my Dougal about Haston and his scarf; it's just the sort of cosmic near-coincidence he loves. For Christmas I gave both sons snow shovels, avalanche probes, reflective emergency tarps, and new headlamps. Avalanche beacons. We study the avalanche reports online every day. I don't tell them this, but I'd rather go like Whillans, quietly, in my sleep.

2014

I did not intend to suggest that I don't particularly like Jim Perrin's biography of Don Whillans, *The Villain*. On the contrary, I think it is the best biography of a climber that we have. My arguments with it, as voiced in this essay, are mere quibbles, points for discussion.

IN THE VERY BIG
ICE HOUSE

Travels on the Harding Icefield

But not yet have we solved the incantation of this whiteness, and learned why it appeals with such power to the
soul; and more strange and far more portentous—why,
as we have seen, it is at once the most meaning symbol
of spiritual things, nay, the very veil of the Christian's
deity; and yet, should be as it is, the intensifying agent
in things the most appalling to mankind.

—Herman Melville, *Moby-Dick*, chapter 42

Five friends are wondering about the size and shape
of the earth. They go exploring and end up walking
through the never-ending passages of a huge ice house
for years and years. Only one of them survives this
ordeal, and when he returns to his people, he reports:
"The earth is simply a very big ice house." Then he dies.

—Inuit creation myth

I.

"Men wanted for hazardous journey, small wages, bitter cold, long months of complete darkness, constant danger, safe return in doubt, honor and recognition in case of success." This probably apocryphal ad is said to have been placed by Ernest Shackleton, the polar explorer, recruiting for his Antarctic journey on the *Endurance*, which would become trapped and slowly crushed by the expanding ice pack in 1915. Shackleton's reputation rests mostly on the fact that, despite the expedition's not setting foot on solid ground for 497 days, no lives were lost.

On the Harding Icefield we hoped to experience few hazards. Certainly our safe return was expected, and the danger, we hoped, would be less than constant. On the other hand, there would be no wages, nor recognition. Any honor would be deeply personal. Craig and I conceived of this expedition under the influence of an interminable Seward rain and whiskey. Between us we convinced John, Q, and Sarah to sign on. It is questionable whether they would join us another time.

II.

The Harding Icefield is the largest ice field wholly located within the United States. It measures one thousand square miles if you include the forty glaciers that flow off it. Ice fields are larger than alpine glaciers, smaller than ice sheets, and similar in area to ice caps. The idea that mineral deposits beneath the ice wield a magnetic force that renders traditional compasses deeply unreliable is somehow appealing. Warren Harding was the first U.S. president to visit Alaska, on a trip called the Voyage of Understanding in 1923, which ended in his death. For many years judged the worst president, due largely to the Teapot Dome scandal, he was the first president whose administration was bought off by big oil interests. He has recently slid to third worst.

III.

The day we left Anchorage in our ancient minivan was the sixtieth anniversary of the day Tenzing Norgay and Edmund Hillary became the first persons to stand on the summit of Everest. That date resonated doubly with me, as it reminded me that within days I too would be sixty years old. On our first trip up the Exit Glacier trail, we had very heavy loads, and the snow was deep and sugary. We were headed for what we would hyperbolically call Advanced Base Camp (our base camp was situated within walking distance of Thorn's Showcase Lounge in downtown Seward). I was breaking through the surface of the snow, postholing, often. Occasionally the holes I punched through filled with wet snow and set up like cement, encasing my boots in ice. A moment of panic ran down my spine before I gathered my wits enough to dig out. Once when I was out in front, I heard Sarah yelling from behind me, "What? What?" I hadn't been talking; I was grunting.

IV.

As we ferried enormous loads up the trail for the second time, we approached the first tiny, snowless patch of ground, where Craig and Sarah were ecstatic about their wolverine sighting. Though late to the event, we could see the animals in their flight from humanity, sprinting, but not quite in a straight line, across the Exit Glacier, like negative images of satellites traversing the night sky.

V.

Craig is always speculating, "What would the Beringians do?," the Beringians being the humans of long ago who traveled from Russia across the Bering land bridge to what is now Alaska. What would they do, and why would they do it? Several days into this speculation, Sarah observes: "People do shit."

VI.

A day or two after the fact, John, with whom I have climbed since 1971, learned via satellite phone that his mother had died on May 31. At the time of her death, he was poised on top of a rocky overlook after scouting an access route from the Exit Glacier to the ice field. From there we could see all the way across the ice field to Truuli Peak, the highest peak on the ice field and a onetime objective of the expedition.

VII.

In every family, and thus many expeditions, the good ones anyway, a private language, an idiolect, evolves. The private and publicly forbidden idiolects of this expedition involved the minivan, Borat, rap songs, and Arnold Schwarzenegger. Sarah and Q wrapped in down, tentbound, chanting, "We're in a tent, mothafocka, we're in a tent." Under no other circumstances would any of us have laughed at this stuff. You had to be there.

VIII.

We had been pinned down in our tents by a whiteout for going on two days, the clouds hugging the ice. We were running out of time, and we began to debate whether we should, as we had been advised, try to wait it out, or move tentatively forward by GPS, fifty feet at a time into the ether.

One advantage we held was that daylight would not be a factor. We would have all the light we needed. But in a whiteout, the light illuminates only itself.

Late in the day it was decided, but not at all unanimously, that we would break camp and push, blindly, deeper onto the ice field.

We broke camp in an hour, faster than we had expected, the mood buoyed immediately by this reversal of inertia. For the first time the terrain would be level enough for sleds, and we would be traveling on skis, escaping our self-imposed quarantine in the tents.

We set off into the whiteness.

To our great delight, the sleds pulled easily. Then, very early into the work, the whiteout began to swirl away. The clouds lifted theatrically, a curtain raised by an unseen hand. For the first time we knew by more than faith (and GPS) where we were. We were on the largest ice field in the United States, and we were approaching its middle. Now, in every direction we could see to its edges, and in between, nunataks rose like islands of rock out of the ocean of whiteness.

It was evening now, and the long Alaskan twilight illuminated the scene with a preternatural clarity. When we stopped and set up the tents and made hot drinks we were thrilled to be there, and we ate dinner and sipped Scotch until the sun sank down to, but not beneath, the horizon, cradled in a valley between two peaks. The ice field was saturated in this deep golden sunlight, and we stayed out in it, blessed by light and luck, until the cold drove us into the tents.

IX.

The word *nunatak* is loan word of Inuit origin (*nunataq*) that refers to a mountain peak rising from and surrounded by glacial ice. It was first used in English in 1882 by J. D. Whitney, who wrote: "The camp was made at the foot of a nunatak, the summit of which was 4,960 feet above the sea-level." The camp to which he referred was in Greenland, and the Inuit first lent the word to the Danish explorers, from whom Whitney borrowed it, permanently. They are called *loan words*, but I doubt permission was asked, language being the least of what was "borrowed." Other Inuit loanwords include *anorak, igloo, kayak*.

X.

Craig had a faded copy of a USGS topographical map with handwritten notes scribbled on it. We were on top of the nunatak known informally by the note maker as the Mule when Q's ski, not leashed to his boot, escaped from him. Echoes of his earlier query, "What are these straps for?," were still ringing in our ears. The ski slid off the summit, at first in slow motion; it picked up velocity and was soon out of sight. I skied after it for approximately one mile, and it was still moving when I swooped in front of it and stopped its downward progress. That's one way of learning where exactly the fall line is. And a lovely run.

XI.

Ernest Hemingway opens "The Snows of Kilimanjaro" with the sighting of a leopard on top of the mountain: "No one has explained what the leopard was seeking at that altitude." On the top of the nunatak, at an altitude of 4,815 feet, we saw a line of raven tracks in the snow. But there was no real mystery to this: nunataks have long been thought to be biological refuges for flora and fauna. From the top of 4,815 we could see down to the Resurrection River Valley and the green riparian corridor that to any ice-field traveler would suggest life. What we were doing there on top of 4,815 is less easily explained.

XII.

On the way down from Camp 2 back to Advanced Base Camp we didn't retrace our steps, didn't go near Camp 1. This was because we had left it in a whiteout, and we could now see that Camp 1 was nowhere near where we thought we were when we set it up. In fact, it was shockingly off any direct route would have been, navigating by global positioning system not yet being an exact science, at least not in our hands. Several skiable lines appeared on the peaks between Camp 1 and ABC. If only I had known they were there.

XIII.

As on almost every other day, on our last, we started late. We wrestled what was left of two loads down in a single load, first by sleds and then, when they became unmanageable, by loading up everything on our backs and just muscling the still-enormous mass of stuff down the trail. If we wondered where the morning had gone, so did we wonder where the nine days had gone. We hit town on the last day of my sixth decade, and it too, the decade, had gone the way of the ice field, into the great whiteout of memory.

2013

For another view of this trip, check out my friend Craig Child's version in his book *Where the World Begins: First People, First Prey, and the Journey into Ice Age North America.*

Illustrations

Acknowledgments

Grateful acknowledgment is made to the publications in which the following pieces first appeared:

"Warnings against Myself," in *Summit* (Fall 1993).

"Speaking in Code," in *The Climbing Art,* no. 16 (1990).

"Climber as Writer: From the Armchair to the Tetons," in *Ascent* (AAC Press, 1990).

"Last Dance of the Wu Li Master: A Distanced Appreciation of Mugs," in *Mountain Review* (U.K.), no. 6 (January–February 1994).

"Virga," in *Isotope: A Journal of Literary Nature and Science Writing,* no. 1.2 (Fall–Winter 2003).

"Untethered in Yosemite: A Report from Paradise in the Last Summer of the Millennium," in *Weber Studies* 20, no. 2 (Winter 2003). Reprinted in *Contact* (University of Nevada Press, 2009).

"Axe of Contrition," in *Alpinist,* no. 20 (Summer 2007).

"Byron Glacier, June 24, 2009," in *Alpinist,* no. 29 (Winter 2009–10).

"Eros on the Heights," in *Cimarron Review,* no. 171 (Spring 2010).

"The Tower and the Riddle," in *Alpinist,* no. 37 (Winter 2011–12).

"Lives of the Volcano Poets," in *Alpinist,* no. 40 (Autumn 2012).

"Here Comes Ol' Flattop," in *Cold Flashes: Literary Snapshots of Alaska,* edited by Michael Engelhard (Fairbanks: University of Alaska Press, 2010).

"A Short Cultural History of the Ice-Axe in the Twentieth Century," in *Ascent,* no. 210 (2013).

✕

These essays were written over many years, and the number of people without whom these could never have been written is enormous. Thanks to kind editors, loyal friends, generous teachers, dedicated students, and of course, partners in the mountains, particularly:

Thanks to Regan Huff, Jacqueline Volin, and Erika Búky of the University of Washington Press for their faith in this project and for their incredible work in bringing this book into being.

Thanks to the editors who first published these essays throughout the years: John Harlin III, David Mazel, Steve Roper and Alan Steck, Jeff Jackson and Alison Osius, Ed Douglas, Chris Cokinas, Brad L. Roghaar, Christian Beckwith, Katie Ives, Jon Billman, and Michael Engelhard.

Thanks to Katie Ives and Jon Waterman for all kinds of support over the years.

For help with the images, thanks to Vered Mares, John McInerney, Craig Childs, and Sean O'Grady.

Thanks again to Dustin Lynx and Jerry Auld of the Imaginary Mountain Surveyors for taking a chance on my first book, *Letters from Chamonix*. I would also like to thank again every person I acknowledged in that book: Drago Archer, Tama Baldwin, Rick Bass, Dave Bean, Monica Berlin, Jerry Brennan, Francois Camoin, Ron Carlson, Anne Caston, Fred Chappell, Mick DeGiulio, Jason Eisert, George Harrison, Barb Harroun, Justin Herrmann, Jack Hicks, Scott Kiefer, David Kranes, Jeff Long, Dan Mancilla, John Mann, Jo-Ann Mapson, Linda McCarriston, Kevin Mellor, the late Hal Moore, Roy Plaeger-Brockway, Skip Raebeck, David Roberts, James Salter (we'll miss you), Ed Schechter, Jeff Schiff, Margaret Schonhofen, Michael Schonhofen, Sherry Simpson, Gary Snyder, Jim Sweeney, Charlie Teske, Randy Thueme, Thomas Jefferey Vasseur, Bernie Wood, Esq., David Wright (where are you, by the way?).

I am particularly grateful to all my climbing partners who appear in this book, too numerous to name individually, and particularly to John McInerney, with whom I first set into the mountains in 1971. Charlie Sassara doesn't appear in these essays, but I'm thankful to him for a tight rope and a quick smile and basically for keeping me alive.

The love and companionship in the mountains of my sons, Macklin Stevenson and Dougal Stevenson, has meant the world to me. As this book was going to press, Macklin passed away suddenly after a too brief twenty-two years lived with blazing intensity. The hole in our hearts where we once held him dear is larger than he ever could have imagined. "Shine on, you crazy diamond."

Dougal: For us there will be more fine days in the mountains. Please check your harness and double-up on all your anchors. Be mindful that there is no shame in turning back and living to climb another day.

In Ann Beattie's story "Snow," a character says, "Any life will seem dramatic if you omit mention of most of it." I have indeed here omitted most of it, and what I have left out, in fact, matters most: a special thanks and love to my wife Aisha Barnes, partner in the grandest adventure of all.